Praise for *Cries from the Cross*

The crucifixion of Jesus Christ brings us face to face with two seemingly contrary attributes of God—His love and His wrath, with two seemingly contradictory doctrines— the sovereignty of God and the free will of man. Once we understand Calvary, we can understand what it is to deny ourselves, take up our cross daily and follow Him. This is a work we should all read.

—**KAY ARTHUR**, Precept Ministries

With his unique insights and careful devotion to the text, Erwin Lutzer takes us deep into the mysteries of the incarnation, no more powerfully revealed than in our Lord's seven statements from the cross. This is not just compelling reading; this is divinely profound truth.

—**JOHN MACARTHUR**, Grace Community Church

Cries from the Cross is truly a journey into the heart of Jesus. It has always been difficult for me to read the words of Jesus from the cross without being overwhelmed by the great love He expressed in His dying moments. You owe it to yourself to read it. Your devotional life will never be the same!

—**DR. DAVID JEREMIAH**, Senior Pastor,
Shadow Mountain Community Church

CRIES FROM THE CROSS

A Journey into the Heart of Jesus

ERWIN W. LUTZER

MOODY PUBLISHERS

CHICAGO

Unless otherwise indicated, Scripture quotations are from The Holy Bible, English Standard Version® (ESV®), copyright © 2001 by Crossway, a publishing ministry of Good News
Publishers. Used by permission. All rights reserved.

Scripture quotations marked NIV are taken from the Holy Bible, New International Ver-
sion®, NIV®. Copyright © 1973, 1978, 1984, 2011 by Biblica, Inc.™ Used by permission
of Zondervan. All rights reserved worldwide. www.zondervan.com. The "NIV" and "New
International Version" are trademarks registered in the United States Patent and Trademark
Office by Biblica, Inc.™

Scripture quotations marked NKJV are taken from the *New King James Version*®. Copyright
© 1982 by Thomas Nelson. Used by permission. All rights reserved.

Scripture quotations marked KJV are taken from the King James Version.

Interior design: Erik M. Peterson
Cover design: Smartt Guys design
Cover image of cross copyright © by Prixel Creative / Lightstock / 127065.
All rights reserved.

Library of Congress Cataloging-in-Publication Data

Lutzer, Erwin W.
Cries from the cross: a journey into the heart of Jesus / Erwin W. Lutzer
       p. cm.
Includes bibliographical references.
ISBN-13: 978-0-8024-1311-6
  1. Jesus Christ—Seven last words—Meditations. I. Title.

BT457 .L88 2002
232.96'35—dc21

                        2001044967

We hope you enjoy this book from Moody Publishers. Our goal is to provide high-quality,
thought-provoking books and products that connect truth to your real needs and challenges. For more information on other books and products written and produced from a
biblical perspective, go to www.moodypublishers.com or write to:

Moody Publishers
820 N. LaSalle Boulevard
Chicago, IL 60610

1 3 5 7 9 10 8 6 4 2

For Jesus, my beloved Savior,
whose death on the cross reconciled me to God
and won my heart.

"May I never boast except
in the cross of our Lord Jesus Christ,
through which the world has been crucified to me,
and I to the world."

GALATIANS 6:14 NIV

CONTENTS

PREFACE

There is a story about a pilgrim making his way to the Promised Land. He was carrying his master's cross, a burden he cheerfully accepted. However, he soon noticed that the farther he walked, the heavier it became. As the pilgrim became weary, he sat down to rest and noticed a woodsman nearby. "Good Friend," the pilgrim called, "could I use your axe to shorten my cross?" The woodsman complied.

The pilgrim traveled on, making much progress. His cross was shorter, his burden lighter. Soon the Promised Land was in sight. Drawing near, however, he noticed that a deep gulf separated him from the glories beyond. He would use the cross to span the chasm.

Though he struggled mightily to lay the cross across the deep rift, it fell short by the very amount he had cut off. Just then the pilgrim awoke; it was a dream. And now, with tears streaming down his face, he clutched his cross to his breast and pressed on. The cross was just as heavy, but now he bore it with more joy. He would endure, all the way to the Promised Land.

Of course we do not enter heaven because we carry a heavy cross but by trusting Christ alone for our salvation. But that said, we as the redeemed are called to carry our cross if we are to have an abundant entrance into the Heavenly Realms. Blessed are those who carry its full weight.

A. W. Tozer was right when he said, "That part of us that we rescue from the cross is the seat of our troubles." The part of the cross we refuse to carry is the part that makes us ineffective for the kingdom of God. The lighter our cross, the weaker our witness.

This book is written with the conviction that the better we grasp what the cross meant to Christ, the better we will understand what the cross should mean to us. We shall learn that for Him the cross meant something quite different from the sentimental notions that often accompany an icon worn around our necks. To stand at the foot of the cross is to witness the purpose for which God created the world. Here we see the attributes of God on display; and if we look carefully, we will see ourselves, with all of our needs, sins, and self-deceptions. Thankfully, it is at the cross that God chose to remove His wrath from those who would humbly trust Christ as their sin-bearer.

No one feels qualified to write a book on the cross. I undertook this task knowing full well that I could only probe the mystery, not fathom it. I could ponder the words of Jesus, but only faintly grasp what they meant to Him in the hour of His suffering. I could visualize the scene, but I struggled to search out its meaning. Thankfully, partial knowledge is still true knowledge; we do not have to understand everything in order to understand something. Thus, any study of the cross brings great personal rewards.

Many of the ideas presented here were derived from my study of other books that have contributed to my understanding of the Seven Sayings of Jesus. I'm indebted to men such as Arthur Pink, Charles Spurgeon, and John Stott, to name a few. A sermon series delivered at Moody Church by Pastor Warren Wiersbe back in 1978, also gave me additional insights, many of which are included. I can only hope that I have paid adequate tribute to these and other men, knowing that in some instances the sources for my ideas may have been either overlooked or forgotten. A book is actually the sum total of inspiration and thoughts derived from years of thought and study.

This book is offered to you as a gift from my heart to yours. If you should find yourself blessed, encouraged, and challenged, the thanks goes to the One who is most worthy of praise. "And they sang a new song, saying: 'You are worthy to take the scroll and to open its seals, because you were slain, and with your blood you purchased for God persons from every tribe and language and people and nation. You have made them to be a kingdom and priests to serve our God, and they will reign on the earth'" (Revelation 5:9–10 NIV).

We join our voices with Fanny Crosby:

> *Jesus, keep me near the cross,*
> *There a precious fountain*

Free to all—a healing stream,
Flows from Calvary's mountain.

In the cross, in the cross,
Be my glory ever;
Till my raptured soul shall find
Rest beyond the river.[1]

The Moody Church
May 2015

A JOURNEY INTO
THE HEART OF JESUS

*And when they had mocked him, they stripped
him of the robe and put his own clothes on him and
led him away to crucify him.*

—MATTHEW 27:31

W ere you there when they crucified my Lord?"
As a child I wondered what those words could possibly mean. Obviously, the author of the hymn intended that we answer yes to the question. And yet, what could be clearer than the fact that I was *not* there when they crucified my Lord? I was born centuries after Jesus died; I missed the event by two millennia. Nor was I there when "they laid Him in the tomb" and when "He rose up from the grave."

Yet, as I have grown in my understanding of the faith, I realize that I *was* there. In fact, if I had not been there, I would not be redeemed. For it was on Calvary that Jesus became legally guilty of my sin. Thanks to His eternal purpose, I can say that He died for me, and that having made purification for my sins, "he sat down at the right hand of the Majesty on high" (Hebrews 1:3). That means that those who weren't *there* will die in their sins.

The cross is widely misunderstood in our day. This can be proven by the fact that it is well-nigh impossible to find anyone who will say anything bad about it. The cross is worn as a pendant by athletes, New Agers, and rock stars. This instrument of indescribable cruelty and death is now a symbol of unity, tolerance, and spirituality of every kind. The "offense of the cross," as Paul put it, has long since vanished as its message is reinterpreted to fit the modern mind. Many who wear the cross around their necks would be scandalized if they understood its meaning.

For example, let me introduce you to a "thirtysomething" woman on a plane en route to Cleveland. My wife and I were sitting together when I noticed that the woman across the aisle from me was wearing a necklace with a cross. Hoping to stimulate a discussion, I said to her, "Thanks for wearing that cross . . . we really do have a wonderful Savior, don't we?"

Surprised, she rolled her eyes upward and responded, "Well, I don't think that I understand the cross like you do—look at this." She held the small cross in her hand and showed me that beneath it was a Jewish Star of David and next to it was a trinket that symbolized the Hindu god Om. "I'm in social work. The people I work with find God in different ways. Christianity is just one of the paths to the divine."

You can imagine the lively discussion we had for the next twenty minutes on whether the cross can be combined with the other religions of the world. I explained that the cross can be united with other symbols on a necklace but never in reality. The better she understood the cross, the more clearly she would see that it must of necessity stand alone. To combine it with any other religion, philosophy, or human idea is to destroy its meaning. I discovered once more that the world at large is deeply offended by the message of the cross. The better the populace understands what Jesus did and why, the more the cross is despised.

Some who want to be known as Christians interpret the cross as the highest tribute to human value. They reason thus: Since God was willing to send His Son to die for us, that must mean that we are of great worth as persons. Therefore, we must use the cross as a means of affirming our dignity and bolstering our self-esteem. Thus, without losing any self-respect, a man can reason that he has a right to be blessed by God simply by virtue of who he (the man) is. Such a cross will not be an offense to anyone, nor will it be branded as foolishness. I'm reminded of a sign on a vendor's table during a festival in Brazil: Cheap Crosses for Sale.

Such people miss the central message of the cross. It is not just that Jesus died for us, but how He died that is important. The cross was not merely a cruel form of death, but it humiliated its victims; it was used to execute those who were most cursed. The procedure with all of its torture ended with the victim naked, with no rights, no reputation, and no recourse. Thus the cross not only proves the gracious love of God toward sinners but also the depth of our sin and rebellion against Him. For us to love sin would be like loving the knife that was used to kill a child.

Listen to every word of Sir Robert Anderson, who wrote this powerful statement: "The cross has shut up man to grace or judgment. It has broken down all 'partition walls' and left a world of naked sinners trembling on the brink of hell. Every effort to recover themselves is but a denial of their doom, and a denial too of the grace of God, which stoops to bring them blessing where they are and as they are."[1] The cross properly understood exalts no one whom it first does not humble; it gives life only to those whom it first "puts to death." The cross exposes the futility of our self-righteousness; it reminds us that we are sinners, incapable of bringing about our own reconciliation with God. Before the cross we can only stand with bowed heads and a broken spirit.

Yes, we were there when our Lord was crucified. Herbert Butterfield wrote:

> The Crucifixion, however else we may interpret it, accuses human nature, accuses us of the very things that we think are our righteousness. . . . Our attitude to the Crucifixion must be that of self-identification with the rest of human nature—we must say, "We did it"; and the inability to adopt something of the same attitude in the case of twentieth-century events has caused our phenomenal failure to deal with the problem of evil.[2]

Unless we see ourselves as deserving of the verdict that Pilate gave to Jesus, unless we see ourselves as worthy of hell, we will never understand the cross. Someone has said that it is difficult for us to embrace the cross in a day when personal enjoyment is king.

Contrary to popular belief, the central message of Christianity is not the Sermon on the Mount or Jesus' parables about love toward one's neighbor. The message that changed the first-century world was that human beings are guilty, helplessly guilty of sins for which they cannot atone. The cross shatters all pride and undercuts the ultimate value of self-effort. The cross stands as proof of God's great love but also reveals our own ugliness. Incredibly, the disciples proclaimed that this cruel, humiliating execution of Jesus was God's most wondrous saving event. No wonder it was a stumbling block to the religious people and foolishness to those who deemed themselves wise! And no wonder it changed their world!

Others misinterpret the cross as a banner to be championed, not as a means of death. Today we are awash with what might be called "cultural Christianity," a kind of teaching that wraps the cross of Christ in the American flag or the flag of some other nation. In our country, these well-meaning people equate the American dream with God's dream for this nation. Thus there is a Christian political agenda, with nationalistic overtones regarding defense, freedom of religion, and boycotts of various kinds. However worthy these goals, by identifying such initiatives as "Christian," we have often clouded the one message that the world needs to hear with clarity and power. Ask any average American what Christians believe and he will give you multiple answers, often reflecting political agendas. Few know that the central doctrine of Christianity is that Christ died on the cross to rescue sinners from an eternal fate.

Have we (I speak to those of us who are committed Christians) forgotten that God's power is more clearly seen in the message of the cross than in any political or social plan we might devise? Might not our search for some antidote to our grievous ills be symptomatic of our lost confidence in the power of the cross to save people from the inside out? Do we cling to the cross with deep conviction that is not simply a part of our message but, correctly understood, the whole of it?

And herein comes the warning. P. T. Forsythe, when

speaking of the cross as the focal point of God's work for sinners, wrote, "If you move faith from that centre, you have driven *the* nail into the Church's coffin. The Church, then, is doomed to death, and it is only a matter of time when she shall expire."[3] The church can only live and breathe at the cross; without it, there is no life and no reason to exist. Properly proclaimed, it is "the power of God unto salvation."

Others think of the cross with deep sentimentality but without a spirit of repentance. In a hospital waiting room I met a woman who was meditating on the wounds of Jesus, with a pendant of the crucified Christ in her hands. "He suffered so much . . . it is unbelievable," she said with tears in her eyes. I reminded her that Jesus suffered for our sins. "Yes," she replied, "but why so *much* suffering? Suffering for a few little lies we tell and a few things we do wrong?"

This lady—bless her—wept over the sufferings of Jesus on the cross but not over her sins that put Him there. As best I could, I explained that if we understood the holiness of God, we would not speak about "little lies" and "a few things we do wrong." For one thing, most people have more than just a few "little" transgressions in their résumé. For another, the first commandment reads, "Love the Lord your God with all your heart and with all your soul and with all your mind and with all your strength" (Mark 12:30). These words condemn us all, for by nature we are preoccupied with our own interests. Only if we think of God as an extension of ourselves would we conclude that our sin is not serious.

Ravi Zacharias said that a new convert wrote to him saying that whenever she read about the cross, it brought her to her knees, thinking about the love of God. But when she read about hell, she became angry with God. She apparently did not realize that we cannot understand the cross unless we understand hell. Without hell, the cross is emptied of its meaning.

Jesus' suffering was terrible for the simple reason that our sin is terrible. And we must ever keep in mind that the suffering of Jesus was not primarily physical—it was not the lacerations, the crown of thorns, and the nails. The spiritual suffering He endured when His fellowship with the Father was broken for three hours on the cross was the ultimate suffering, the kind of agony you and I have never experienced.

Keep in mind that crucifixion—for all of its horrors—was common in the first century. It is estimated that the Romans crucified thirty thousand people a year. This was the accepted form of death for political prisoners and criminals of various sorts. These men endured the same physical suffering as Jesus. But the cup that the Father gave Christ to drink; that cup meant that He would become our "sin bearer." The horror of our Savior's holiness coming in contact with our sinfulness is what Calvary was all about.

GOD'S VIEW OF THE CROSS

The cross was, above all else, for God the Father. Paul wrote, "God presented Christ as a sacrifice of atonement, through faith in his blood . . . He did this to demonstrate his righteousness . . . at the present time, so as to be just and the one who justifies those who have faith in Jesus" (Romans 3:25–26 NIV).

In Old Testament times God had fellowship with the likes of Abraham, Moses, and David, along with countless others whose sins had not yet been finally put away. Since the blood of animals was only symbolic, God chose to save these people on credit; He set aside their sin so that He could have fellowship with them, but the ransom had not yet been paid. Thus, to make sure that no one could question His justice, Christ died to make the payment for them and also for us.

The obedience of Christ as the Lamb of God was precious to the Father. Paul says we are to live a life of love, "as Christ loved us and gave himself up for us, a fragrant offering and sacrifice to God" (Ephesians 5:2). The willingness of the Son to suffer according to an agreed-upon plan was a fragrant offering and a pleasing sacrifice to God.

God took delight in the sacrifice of His Son. "Yet it was the LORD's will to crush him and cause him to suffer, and though the LORD makes his life an offering for sin, he will see his offspring and prolong his days, and the will of the LORD will prosper in his hand" (Isaiah 53:10 niv). If we ask the question, Who put Jesus to death? our first response should not be "the Jews" or "Pilate" but "God." God crushed His Son. Peter says He was handed over to the Jews "according to the definite plan and foreknowledge of God" (Acts 2:23). To put it plainly, in concert with the Father's plan, *Jesus got Himself crucified.*

Did God whip His Son and put the nails through His hands and feet? No, to be sure, this cruelty was done by wicked men. And yet these sinners did what God purposed to be done. We must accept as a fact the mystery that the blame for Jesus' death belongs to the evil people; and yet, the plan was God's. Peter, speaking of all the players who conspired to crucify Jesus, said, "They did what your power and will had decided beforehand should happen" (Acts 4:28 niv).

Why would the Father do such a thing? John Piper answers, "He did it to resolve the dissonance between his love for his glory and his love for sinners."[4] God could not simply let bygones be bygones. Thus, before time began, God the

Father and God the Son agreed upon a plan in which the iniquity of us all would be laid upon Jesus; He would bear our punishment so that we could be justly acquitted by God the Father. Sin would be shown to be the horrible thing it is, and God would be shown to be the loving God He is. At the cross His inflexible holiness collided with His love to the mutual satisfaction of each attribute.

Today we often hear it said that God forgives people on the basis of His love rather than on the basis of His atoning sacrifice. Modern minds, having rationalized their sins, find it difficult to understand that God cannot extend His grace toward sinners until His holy justice is satisfied. Just yesterday, I was told that it was arrogant to suggest that a well-known leader of an Eastern religion (an obviously good man) would be barred from entry into heaven. But the scriptural answer is this: Only those who have been shielded from God's wrath by the death of Christ shall be saved. Or, to put it more positively, only those who have the righteousness of the crucified Christ credited to them will be given entrance into God's presence.

Even in heaven, the cross will be remembered. When John was allowed a glimpse into heaven, he told us that he wept because no one was found who could open the book that represented the title deed to the universe. He continued:

> Then one of the elders said to me, "Do not weep! See, the Lion of the tribe of Judah, the Root of David, has triumphed. He is able to open the scroll and its seven seals."
>
> Then I saw a Lamb, looking as if it had been slain, standing at the center of the throne, encircled by the four living creatures and the elders. (REVELATION 5:5–6 NIV)

A lamb, *looking as if it had been slain!*

Martin Luther often struggled with doubt and with the devil. He was well aware of how easily we are deceived because of a story about St. Martin, the figure in history after whom Luther was named. The story goes that St. Martin had a vision of Christ. But when he glanced at His hands, to make sure they had nail prints, the apparition disappeared. So he never knew whether he had encountered Christ or the devil.

There are many "christs" today, but they lack nail prints. We have teachers and gurus who tell us how to live happier and more productive lives. We are told how we can get "in touch with the deepest part of ourselves" and how we can be spiritual without being religious. What millions do not have, however, is a God with wounds, a God who entered into our world and suffered on our behalf so that we might be reconciled to the Almighty. So important is this central act of redemption that it changed the unchangeable; indeed, heaven is different because of "the lamb who was slain." The blood is gone, but the scar remains as a reminder of our sin and a reminder of His grace.

> *I shall know Him, I shall know Him,*
> *And redeemed by His side I shall stand*
> *I shall know Him, I shall know Him*
> *By the print of the nails in His hand.*[5]

No one can experience the eternal favor of God if they bypass the cross. The cross is the hinge upon which the door of history swings. It is the hub that holds the spokes of God's purposes in a grand unity. The Old Testament prophets pointed toward it and the New Testament disciples proclaimed it. When we "cling to the old rugged cross," as the familiar hymn encourages us to do, we are not doing so out of mere sentimentality. The cross is the heart of our message and the heart of our power to combat the encroaching darkness.

CRIES FROM THE CROSS

Last words are always important. But surely there can be no last words as significant as those of Jesus on the cross. Here we see His heart, His love for His people whom He was redeeming. In these cries we see the humanity of Jesus. His wounds were not bandaged so that ours might be; His sorrows were great so that our sorrows might be taken away. Isaiah described Him: "His appearance was so disfigured beyond that of any human being and his form marred beyond human likeness" (Isaiah 52:14 NIV). He could not be recognized as being the person He was. He was the victim of false accusations and violence. His antagonists urged the Romans to get rid of Him. And now His enemies felt vindicated when they saw the nails, smelled the blood, and heard the groans.

Imagine Him stripped and bound by the wrists to a column in Pilate's court, then scourged with thongs containing balls of lead or bone chips. As they pound against His body, beads of blood form that with repeated blows break open into wounds. Then the crown of thorns is pressed into His head and blood mingles with His matted hair. He tries to carry His cross, but when He staggers, Simon of Cyrene is pressed to help Him. At Calvary He is stripped of His cloths and "excruciating pain, like millions of hot needles, shock the nervous system." Then He is hoisted onto the cross itself as the executioners pound long square nails into His palms.

By having the great nerve centers wounded, He experiences "the most unbearable pain a man can experience. . . . Each movement of the body revives this horrible pain."[6]

Even while in agony, Jesus was yet a King. But He turns our views of greatness upside down. Read the words of Brooke Foss Wescott carefully:

> The sovereignty of Christ from the cross is a new sovereignty. It has destroyed forever the formula that might is right. It has put to shame the self-assertion of false heroism. It has surrounded with imperishable dignity the completeness of sacrifice. It has made clear to the pure heart that the prerogative of authority is wider service. The divine King rules forever by dying.[7]

Here is an answer for those who ask, "Where was God when . . . ?" Come with me into my study and let us listen to the story of a young woman, abused by her father and thrown quite literally into the streets at age fourteen. Now that she had come to trust Christ as her Savior, she asked, "Where was God when I was lonely and hurting? Where was He when my alcoholic father woke us at 3:00 a.m. and beat us mercilessly on our beds?" Then she added, "I know God is my Father, but it seems as if He was absent when I needed Him the most."

Gently, I took her on a journey into the heart of Jesus. In the suffering of the cross, we not only find forgiveness but also healing for our deepest hurts. Just as the cross is an exchange for our sin—our sin is credited to Christ and His righteousness is credited to us—so our emotional burdens are also transferred to His shoulders.

> Surely he has borne our griefs and carried our sorrows;
> yet we esteemed him stricken, smitten by God, and af-
> flicted. But he was pierced for our transgressions; he was
> crushed for our iniquities; upon him was the chastise-
> ment that brought us peace, and with his wounds we are
> healed. (ISAIAH 53:4–5)

He has borne our griefs and sorrows.

That does not mean that we can live in emotional tran-
quility any more than we can live free of sin. But it does
mean that we can be comforted with the sure conviction that
the deepest injustices of humanity were addressed. The cross
was God's farthest reach; it is here that we identify most
closely with Christ. We cannot, of course, duplicate His experience, but we can identify with His wounds. As we shall
learn, Christ was forsaken that we might not be; He experienced hell that we might experience heaven.

Did He die for our physical healing too? Yes, He redeemed all of us—body, soul, and spirit. It would be a mistake,
however, to assume that this means that we can be healed at
any time and that we have a right to "claim our healing." The
Scriptures make it clear that we do not see the completion
of our redemption in this life. Just as He overcame death,
but yet we must endure it, so He purchased our new bodies
that await our resurrection. Those who want everything now
mislead multitudes who fall prey to the "name it claim it"
philosophy. In this life we receive forgiveness of sin and the
Holy Spirit as a down payment of future glory. But heaven is
not yet here; physical healing, though purchased, still awaits.

The cross reminds us that our self-condemnation must
end. We need no longer keep score. We must not believe that
God thinks about us as we think about ourselves. Receiving God's forgiveness and extending forgiveness to others is

both our privilege and responsibility. Richard Foster wrote, "Today the heart of God is an open wound of love. He aches over our distance and preoccupation. He mourns that we do not draw near to him. He grieves that we have forgotten him. He weeps over our obsession with muchness and manyness. He longs for our presence."[8] He was bound for me, lacerated for me, rejected for me, and raised to newness of life for me.

Dietrich Bonhoeffer was right when he said that guilt is an idol some people refuse to give up. We must dare to accept what God offers and not turn Him away. Some people think they are doing God a favor when they refuse His forgiveness, reasoning that He is so mad at them that He does not want to see them anyway. Such people insult God, for they live as though Christ's death were insufficient for their sins. Be assured He is able to save all who choose to believe. His wounds were proof of His love.

See, from His head, His hands, His feet,
Sorrow and love flow mingled down;
Did e're such love and sorrow meet,
Or thorns compose so rich a crown?[9]

My computer immediately underlines all misspelled words with a jagged red line. Sometimes it also underlines words that are spelled correctly, but the red line appears because the words did not find their way into the software program. The computer I'm using does not recognize the word *brokenness*. Unfortunately, many of us don't recognize the word either. We know what it is like to be broke; but we haven't experienced brokenness, a word that reminds us that at the cross all self-aggrandizement ends. Here we are introduced to the mystery of God's providential will for us. Here we come to the end of self-seeking and forever reject the notion that we are worthy to cooperate with God in His salvation.

In Africa, a fire ravaged a hut, burning quickly and intensely, killing all in the family except one. A stranger was seen running into the burning house. He snatched a small boy from the flames, carried him to safety, and then disappeared into the darkness.

The next day the tribe met to decide what should be done with the lad. Perhaps superstitiously, they assumed he must be a special child because he survived the fire. A wise man insisted that he adopt the boy; a rich man thought he was better qualified.

As the discussion ensued, a young, unknown man walked into the middle of the circle and insisted that he had prior claim to the child. He then showed them his hands, freshly burned in the fire of the preceding night. He was the rescuer and therefore insisted that the child was rightfully his. Just so, our scarred Savior claims us.

> *The other gods were strong; but Thou wast weak.*
> *They rode, but Thou didst stumble to thy throne.*
> *But to our wounds only God's wounds can speak,*
> *And not a god has wounds but Thou alone.*[10]

A God with wounds! Jesus was not silent on the cross. As we turn our attention to His cries, we stand on holy ground. His cries reveal the deepest longings of His heart. Here we see His final act of selfless suffering. Join me on a journey that should make us exclaim, "Behold how He loved us!"

CHAPTER 1

A CRY FOR PARDON

*"Father, forgive them, for they
know not what they are doing."*

—LUKE 23:34

How can I forgive him if I can't *trust* him?"

A wife was speaking of her husband, who had an affair with a woman he met on a cruise to the Caribbean. This was not the first time he had strayed, nor the second, but the third. Now he was returning, asking to be forgiven again. Because he was honest in his confession, he expected the forgiveness to be instant, unconditional, and complete. After all, his wife was a Christian, wasn't she?

Forgiveness sounds like a marvelous idea until you are the one who has to do it. How can you forgive someone who keeps breaking a promise? Why should you forgive someone who doesn't ask for it? And why should you be the one to forgive when you are the one who was wronged? Must you forgive someone who is out to destroy you? Perhaps nowhere do we have our questions about forgiveness answered more clearly than at the cross. The Savior's first cry was one for pardon for His enemies.

"Father, forgive them, for they know not what they do" (Luke 23:34).

During His ministry Jesus often forgave those who needed His mercy. "Son, your sins are forgiven," He said to the paralytic (Mark 2:5). His remarks caused a storm of controversy, for His hearers knew that only God could forgive sins. Even sin against others is ultimately sin against God. Jesus explained that He had the right to forgive sins because He had the credentials of deity.

Now, on the cross, He did not exercise this divine prerogative. He asked the Father to do what He had previously done. Sacrificed as the Lamb of God, He refused the role of deity. He was God, to be sure, but chose to suspend His divine rights. He so completely identified with us that He temporarily withdrew Himself from a position of authority. Yet His heart was burdened for those who had instigated and committed history's greatest crime. He prayed that the unforgivable might be forgiven.

In this first cry from the cross, Jesus called God "Father." He shall do so again as He breathes His last: "Father, into your hands I commit my spirit!" (Luke 23:46). But in the middle cry, He will shout, "My *God*, my *God*, why have you forsaken me?" (Mark 15:34, emphasis added). That, as we shall learn, was His darkest hour, so dark that even nature resonated as the light of the sun was blotted out. In that moment, the Son experienced the full penalty for our sins and even the Father withdrew His blessed presence.

He could call God "Father" while being treated unjustly. When the mob arrived at the place called the Skull (Luke 23:33), the cross was laid on the ground and He was lowered on top of it. That is when His prayer began. The Greek text implies that He kept repeating the words *"Father,* forgive them . . ." (Luke 23:34, emphasis added). Though He was arrested illegally and suffered personal insults, He knew that He could count on His Father's blessing and presence. He also knew that His prayer for His enemies would be answered.

All His disciples abandoned Him (except John, who later returned to the scene of the crime). The injustices of His enemies and the betrayal of His friends did not shatter His confidence in the Father's presence. He knew that the Father could have spared Him this injustice; indeed, as the second person of the Trinity, He could have chosen to come down from the cross. But such a deliverance was not part of the plan agreed upon in the eons of eternity. Thus, He was content to say "Father," though His personal rights were arrogantly ignored and insults were hurled at Him. These sufferings did not hide the face of the One whom He sought to please.

The Reverend Warren Wiersbe, former pastor of Moody Church, asked, "Is your faith shaken by the wickedness of sinners or the weakness of saints?"[1] Yes, sometimes our faith is shaken. A woman whose husband had tried to destroy her, poisoning the attitude of their four children against her, said, "I don't see God at all . . . He is nowhere in this." We can identify with her, for we all have, at times, felt abandoned by God. We tell ourselves that no father could watch his child suffer unjustly. But Christ's Father remained firm in the presence of unrestrained wickedness. He knew that He could depend upon His Father, even when evil seemed to be out of control.

When man had done his worst, Jesus prayed, not for justice, but for mercy; He pleaded that His enemies would be exempt from the just consequences of their evil deeds. And He prayed, not after His wounds had healed, but while they were yet open. Words of forgiveness came from His lips when the nails were being driven into His body, when the pain was the fiercest, when the jolts of anguish were the sharpest; He prayed as the cross was lowered into the hole with a thud. It was then, when His nerves were yet the most tender, when the pain was the most unfathomable, He who was the victim of history's greatest crime prayed for the criminals.[2]

He could forgive because He was about His Father's business. In Gethsemane, He prayed, "My Father, if it be possible, let this cup pass from me; nevertheless, not as I will, but as you will" (Matthew 26:39). The cup was not a satanic attack, though Satan no doubt tried to add his own ingredients into the potion given Him. The cup was the one given to Him by His Father. It was the task of purchasing "people for God from every tribe and language and people and nation" (Revelation 5:9). This meant that the Son would be cruelly crucified and become "sin" for humanity. He would drink the cup of suffering to the dregs. This cup would purchase the forgiveness for which He now prayed.

Can we say "Father" when we are being crucified? Can we pray for the forgiveness of those who are trying to destroy us? Do we have enough faith to leave justice in the hands of our heavenly Father? "Beloved, never avenge yourselves, but leave it to the wrath of God, for it is written: 'Vengeance is mine, I will repay,' says the Lord" (Romans 12:19). On the cross we see the restraint of a Man who had the power to destroy but chose instead to forgive.

In these words is the hope of our own deliverance. So let us come near to listen more intently to what is being said. Perhaps we shall hear our own name in the petition.

A PRAYER FOR FORGIVENESS

Surrounded by jeering taunts, weakened by the loss of blood, His lips were moving. What was He trying to say? Was He groaning with pain? Did He mumble words of self-pity? Did He curse those who crucified Him? No, He had a word of forgiveness for His enemies. "Father, forgive them . . ." Though He was personally sinless, He was "numbered with the transgressors" (Isaiah 53:12). Even now, He was bearing their sin and pleading that His sacrifice might be effectively applied to them. Even this was a fulfillment of prophecy. "Yet he bore the sin of many, and makes intercession for the transgressors" (v. 12).

He prayed aloud so that we might know we are included in this prayer. Already the night before in the garden of Gethsemane, He remembered us.

> I do not ask for these only, but also for those who will believe in me through their word, that they may all be one, just as you, Father, are in me, and I in you, that they also may be in us, so that the world may believe that your have sent me. (JOHN 17:20–21)

The prayer begun that evening continued on the cross, and even today He is at the right hand of the Father making intercession for us. Be assured, He will never forget us.

Five bleeding wounds He bears,
Received on Calvary;
They pour effectual prayers,
They strongly plead for me;
"Forgive him, O, forgive," they cry,
"Nor let that ransomed sinner die![3]

Let's move on to the next phrase of the prayer. "Father, forgive them, for they know not what they do" (Luke 23:34). Were they ignorant of their wrongdoing? Of course not. Judas knew he had betrayed a friend; Pilate knew he had condemned an innocent man; the Sanhedrin knew that they bribed false witnesses to make the charges stick. All of these people were not ignorant of the facts of their guilt, but they were ignorant of the *enormity* of their crime. For whatever reason, they did not know that they were crucifying the Son of God.

Paul the apostle agreed. He said that we have hidden wisdom, then added, "None of the rulers of this age understood this, for if they had, they would not have crucified the Lord of glory" (1 Corinthians 2:8). If they had known what is now clear, they would have recognized Jesus to be Messiah, the Lord of glory. Their crime was much greater than they could ever have realized because of the infinite value of the person whom they had condemned. They knew what they had done, but they did not know *all* they had done.

The Old Testament distinguishes sins of ignorance from sins of presumption, that is, sinning with a clenched fist. "But anyone who sins defiantly ... blasphemes the LORD and must be cut off from the people of Israel" (Numbers 15:30 NIV). Such a sin is especially evil since it is committed with knowledge; it is willful and rebellious. In the New Testament

Jesus spoke of an unpardonable sin, that is, a sin committed by the nation Israel in their persistent, deliberate rejection of His messiahship. Obviously, the people had varying degrees of responsibility because they had varying degrees of knowledge. For some the rejection of Christ was willful rebellion.

Contrast this with the sin of ignorance: "If anyone commits a breach of faith and sins unintentionally . . . he shall bring to the LORD as his compensation, a ram without blemish out of the flock" (Leviticus 5:15). Such sins needed a sacrifice, but they were not as serious as willful, defiant rebellion. Even in Old Testament times, God evaluated behavior by the attitude of the heart and the knowledge of the mind.

Don't overlook the fact that even sins of ignorance need forgiveness. Jesus did not say, "They don't know what they were doing, so let them go free." God never lowers His standard of justice to the level of our ignorance. Sins committed in ignorance are still sins. The guilt of those who crucified Jesus was real and objective regardless of how much they understood or did not understand.

Have you ever driven through a red light "ignorantly"? A friend of mine argued with a policeman, trying to make the point that he did not see the stop sign. You can guess who won the argument. Ignorance is no excuse in our society, nor is ignorance an excuse in the presence of God. What is more, those who crucified Jesus *should* have known, and they *would* have known if only they had not feared where the truth might take them.

Contrast their knowledge with ours. They did not know that a resurrection would follow the crucifixion; they did not know that a church that would change the world would grow out of Pentecost; they did not know that a New Testament would be written that spells out in detail God's plan of the ages. I'm often asked whether people of other religions who have not heard about Christ will be saved. Usually, the question comes from those who know much about Christ and can examine His credentials in detail. They seem more concerned about those who have never heard than about their own response to God. But if responsibility is based on knowledge, those who are born in our culture will experience much greater condemnation than those who have never heard.

Certainly all sin makes us ignorant. We have no idea of the greatness of our sin because we do not understand the greatness of our God. But we have fewer excuses today than ever; we have no reason to turn away from the Savior who left us powerful witnesses to His authenticity.

> Since the message declared by angels proved to be reliable, and every transgression or disobedience received a just retribution, how shall we escape if we neglect such a great salvation? . . . God also bore witness by signs and wonders and various miracles and by gifts of the Holy Spirit distributed according to his will. (HEBREWS 2:2–4)

I know a young man who has defiantly chosen to reject Jesus. He was brought up in a fine Christian home and attended Christian schools. His guilt is greater than that of his best friend in college, who grew up without Christian parents, without a church, and without a moral example. Both are guilty; both have every reason to seek Christ; and both are neglecting their salvation, but with differing levels of responsibility. Such people, wrote Arthur Pink, are "blind to their madness."[4]

THE ANSWER TO HIS PRAYER

"Father, forgive them, for they know not what they do."

Was His prayer answered? I'm convinced that Jesus received whatever He asked for. Unlike us, the Son always knew the Father's will, so the Father was always pleased to give His beloved Son His every petition. Forgiveness came to all those for whom Jesus prayed. Of course I don't mean that everyone connected with the crucifixion was forgiven. Many died in their sins, but those for whom the prayer was uttered were forgiven.

"Now we stand as sinners at the foot of his cross," wrote Bonhoeffer, "and now a puzzle difficult to understand is solved: Jesus Christ, the innocent one, prays as God's vengeance on the godless is fulfilled. . . . The one who bore the vengeance, he alone was allowed to ask for the forgiveness of the godless."[5] Here the vengeance of God is turned away so that forgiveness might come from the very One who prays that it be so. In effect, Jesus was praying that His own death would be effective for those for whom it was intended.

Some of the soldiers standing at the foot of the cross were forgiven. The centurion who was probably in charge of the crucifixion ordeal was deeply troubled by the darkness, the earthquake, and the tearing of the veil of the temple. Taking his stand against popular opinion, he exclaimed, "Truly this was the Son of God" (Matthew 27:54 KJV). I expect to see him in heaven.

The Jews in Jerusalem who called for His crucifixion—the ones who, standing before Pilate, shouted, "His blood be on us and on our children!" (Matthew 27:25)—many of them were forgiven. Perhaps we want to argue that they were not ignorant of what they were doing. Surely, we think, these cannot be the people Jesus had in mind. It appears as if they knew *exactly* what they were doing.

Surprisingly, Peter thought they were ignorant of the full extent of their guilt. Listen to him preach: "You killed the Author of life, whom God raised from the dead. . . . Now, brothers, I know that you acted *in ignorance,* as did also your rulers" (Acts 3:15, 17, emphasis added). As a result of his sermon, some two thousand people accepted Jesus as Messiah. We must add this number to the three thousand who responded to the message on the Day of Pentecost to account for the total that swelled to some five thousand (Acts 4:4). We also read that a great number of the temple priests confessed Jesus as Lord (Acts 6:7). All of this in answer to Jesus' prayer!

Reflect on God's mercy! He did not hold the murder of His beloved Son against these criminals! Many proclaimed, "His blood be on us and on our children!" (Matthew 27:25), meaning they would bear the guilt of Jesus' death in future generations. But in God's sovereign mercy, His blood was instead applied to their hearts! Jim Nance observed that He "turned their words around and applied Christ's blood for the far more glorious work of their eternal salvation."[6]

Could God have forgiven these people without their asking to be forgiven? No. The prayer was not for those who did not want to be forgiven, but for those who would seek it. Nor was this a general prayer, giving a blanket pardon to all who were involved in the crucifixion. This was a prayer for those specific individuals whom God would save. We have no evidence that Jesus ever prayed for the world as such, but He did pray for those who were not yet a part of His family but some day would be (John 17:9).

If Jesus had come down from the cross, His prayer could not have been answered. These conversions two thousand years ago were a kind of "firstfruits" in anticipation of the day when all Israel will be saved. And the Gentile conversions were also the "firstfruits," anticipating the day when we who are Gentiles would be welcomed into the kingdom.

OUR QUESTIONS ANSWERED

In this prayer, we have at least some answers to our questions about forgiveness.

Are some sins "unpardonable"? The answer is no, for if the murder of the Son of God was "forgivable" for those who sought forgiveness, then all sins can be forgiven. On February 9, 2001, an American submarine came up above the surface of the water and hit a Japanese fishing vessel, and nine were drowned. Parents who lost a son in the accident were quoted as saying, "What happened was unforgivable." We know what they meant, because sometimes human beings feel a loss so deeply that extending forgiveness is beyond their ability. When a babysitter is responsible for the death of the child, the parents often feel there is too much to forgive. But what man cannot forgive, God can. The cross can repair the irreparable.

A man who raped four women wrote to me asking whether he could be forgiven. My first inclination was to say, "Not if I have anything to do with it!" But the answer is yes, he can be forgiven by God, though he may not experience the forgiveness of the victims whose lives he ruined. He, and a host of others like him, must be content with the forgiveness of God when the forgiveness of man fails. There is no unpardonable sin for those who come to Christ for forgiveness. For those who refuse Him, all sins are unpardonable.

"By this prayer from the cross," writes Clarence Cranford,

"Jesus was building a bridge of forgiveness over which his tormentors could come in penitence to the Father."[7] God did not hold the murder of His precious Son, the Lord of Glory, against those who had the will to believe. Jesus' prayer was answered, because the cross is the self-substitution of God; He who needed no forgiveness died for those of us who are condemned without it.

If you are ever tempted to think that God takes sin lightly, look at Calvary. A friend of mine said he was sharing the gospel with a woman on a plane who felt that she was good enough to go to heaven. When he asked her what she would do if, in fact, her works were not good enough, she responded, "I would tell God that He should lighten up."

Skull Hill, as Calvary was called, reminds us that God can't "lighten up." His searing holiness demanded an infinite penalty. And although God forgives us because of Christ, it is neither His job nor His obligation to do so. He forgives us because of undeserved mercy toward us whose just punishment is hell. The cross is the bridge of redeeming love; on it, we walk across the chasm to God, who graciously provided forgiveness for those who believe. If we do not understand this, we do not understand the gospel.

Should we pray for those who do not ask for our forgiveness? Yes, Jesus prayed for His enemies before they became His friends. Of course we do not know the future response of those for whom we pray. We do not know whether they will seek God's forgiveness, or, for that matter, our forgiveness if they have wronged us. Yet, Jesus taught His disciples to "pray for those who spitefully use you and persecute you" (Matthew 5:44 NKJV). These are Christ's instructions when our enemies do to us what His enemies did to Him. We can pray like Jesus, "Forgive them, for they know not what they do," but unlike Him, we do not know exactly how our prayer will be answered.

Should we forgive those who do not ask for it? Since God does not forgive those who refuse to ask for His forgiveness, why should we? The answer is that when our forgiveness is not requested, we must still grant it in the sense that we release our bitterness to God and commit our adversaries to Him.

In human relationships, when forgiveness is requested, reconciliation is never a certainty. "If your brother sins, rebuke him, and if he repents, forgive him, and if he sins against you seven times in the day, and turns to you seven times, saying, 'I repent,' you must forgive him" (Luke 17:3–4). The goal of forgiveness is always reconciliation, that is, the uniting of two divided hearts. But when forgiveness is not requested, the offended party must still choose to "forgive" in the sense that the injustice is turned over to God. If not, the hurt and anger will destroy the human psyche and grieve the Holy Spirit. The perpetrator has caused enough pain already; the only way to be free from his or her continuing influence is to "forgive" by surrendering the matter to God.

As far as we know, Timothy McVeigh, the Oklahoma City bomber who killed 168 people in 1995, died unforgiven by God and man. There was no reason for the relatives of his victims to grant him the forgiveness he neither wanted nor requested. And yet, among the survivors, those who have been able to "forgive" by trusting God to "even the score" will be rewarded with greater emotional health and stability. Such is the spirit of Jesus.

But where is justice? How can we choose to "forgive" a man who deserves a fate worse than death? How can we surrender the anger that properly seeks compensation and revenge? Jesus helps us here as well. "When he was reviled, he did not revile in return; when he suffered, he did not threaten, but continued entrusting himself to him who judges justly" (1 Peter 2:23). Jesus could forgive without surrendering His desire for justice. He felt no need to even the score at the moment. He committed His plight to the Judge of the universe and could wait for the final verdict.

Two thousand years have passed, and those who mistreated Jesus and rejected His forgiveness—those criminals—have not yet been brought to justice. But a day is coming when they shall stand before the Father of the One they so cruelly wronged. Jesus was content to wait for that day, for His faith in the Father's justice did not waver. Yes, we too can entrust ourselves to Him who judges justly.

The woman whose husband has left her for another lover; the teenager whose childhood was stolen through parental abuse; the brother who was chiseled out of his inheritance by an unscrupulous relative—these, and others like them, must surrender their hurt to God and be content with the sure knowledge that all such cases have yet to be tried by what is truly *the* Supreme Court.

Should we forgive those who ask for forgiveness even when we doubt their sincerity or cannot trust their motives? The answer is yes, for we cannot see the human heart. Jesus told the disciples that they must be willing to forgive many times—seventy times seven—if they wished to understand God's forgiveness. However—and this is important—forgiveness must again be distinguished from reconciliation. A wife can forgive her adulterous husband, but that does not mean that she is required to blindly trust his lifestyle. There has to be counseling, the passing of time, and accountability. Regaining trust is a long, often difficult process.

Where sin is not taken seriously, forgiveness is received too lightly. Even sincere repentance must be updated with daily surrender to God and responsible disciplines. Our entire lives must be characterized by repentance. No one act of repentance in and of itself guarantees a future life of obedience.

The first cry from the cross echoes the one word without which we cannot be saved: *forgiveness*. Then as now, it is freely granted to those who humbly receive it. Thankfully, the death of Jesus made the answer to this prayer a reality.

CHAPTER 2

_____

A CRY OF ASSURANCE

"Today you will be with me in paradise."
—LUKE 23:43

We all find it difficult to speak with the dying; we find it especially difficult to speak to them about their impending death. Nurses tell us that relatives and friends adopt a code of silence, avoiding the one topic that their dying friend might wish to speak about. When a man who had been my doctor lay dying of cancer, I knew that this was not the time for platitudes. As I leaned over his bed, I whispered almost directly into his ear, "Dr. ———, you have to accept Christ as your Savior." To which he replied, "I know I do, but I don't know how."

I know I do, but I don't know how! That afternoon, God

45

gave me the privilege of showing him "how," and in the few weeks he had left, he not only had the assurance of heaven but wanted the Bible read to him. How much better if he had come to faith in Christ early in life, but, thankfully, God's grace is given even to those who are at the threshold of death. Yes, it is better late than never.

If we were the centurion in charge of the crucifixion, we would have put the two thieves next to each other and Jesus off to the side. This Roman soldier probably had no idea why he arranged the crosses as he did, but he was fulfilling an ancient prophecy: "He ... was numbered with the transgressors" (Isaiah 53:12). God decreed that He who was most holy should die with those who were most *un*holy. Jesus not only died among criminals but was numbered as one of them, and therein lies the heart of the gospel.

God had His reasons for decreeing that Jesus should gracelessly hang between two thugs. He wanted to demonstrate the depths of shame to which His Son was willing to descend. At His birth He was surrounded by beasts, and, now, in His death, with criminals. Let no one say that God has stayed aloof from the brokenness of our fallen world. He descended that we might ascend with Him to newness of life. But I'm ahead of the story.

Our attention turns to the two men who were crucified on either side of Him. One particularly holds our attention because he received a promise that we must share if we are to be in paradise with our Lord. Here is assurance for those in our hospital wards dying of cancer; here also is hope for the strong and healthy who will someday face death without warning. Here is hope for the worst of sinners and the best of sinners.

What a day for this thief! In the morning he was justly

crucified on a cross; by late that evening he was justly welcomed into paradise by Jesus!

Let's reflect on the story.

HIS PREDICAMENT

This man's rap sheet shows that he was a career criminal, a "bad to the bone" thief who initially joined with the enemies of Jesus in deriding Him: "And the robbers who were crucified with him also reviled him in the same way" (Matthew 27:44). His attitude was like that of his partner in crime, hanging just on the other side of Jesus. We don't know who was the greater sinner of the two, but either of them could have been on Jerusalem's Most Wanted posters.

Bad as he was, he represents all of us. We might object, arguing that we are not thieves; we are not robbing banks and snatching purses from little old ladies walking down the street. But honesty requires us to admit that we have all robbed God. Suppose you were appointed by a firm in New York to represent its interests in Chicago. Every month they forwarded your check to you, which you gladly signed and cashed. But the fact is that you never worked for the company at all, but served another firm. Would that not be thievery?[1]

That describes us exactly. God gives us life; He gives us talents; He gives us the ability to earn money; He gives us friends; and yet we serve ourselves rather than Him. Rather than bringing glory to God, we live for ourselves and unintentionally serve Satan's selfish interests. If we stopped comparing ourselves among ourselves and held our records next to the face of God, we would see that we are not much better than the thief who joined with his friend in ridiculing Jesus.

This man was out of options. It was too late for a new beginning, too late for hoping that his good deeds would outweigh the bad. Author Arthur Pink put it this way: "He could not walk in the paths of righteousness for there was a nail through either foot. He could not perform any good works for there was a nail through either hand. He could not turn over a new leaf and live a better life for he was dying."[2] Yet helplessness is not a curse if it draws us to the only One who can help us. Indeed, if we are not helpless, we cannot be saved.

There on the cross, this man—bless him—had a change of heart.

HIS REMARKABLE FAITH

Quite possibly, this thief did not see Jesus until that very day. As the three men were being nailed to their crosses, he thought that Jesus was just another criminal. When the crosses were lifted up and lowered into their holes, the thief had no reason to believe that he was in the presence of greatness. Golgotha was where criminals died. It was not a place where one would expect to find a divine man.

What changed his mind? We can surmise that, first, he heard Jesus pray, "Father, forgive them, for they know not what they do" (Luke 23:34). He could not forget those words, for only a man who knew God could pray to the Father for the forgiveness of others. The prayer pierced his conscience, and he realized the stupidity and blindness of his own heart. He knew that he also needed forgiveness.

Then there was the inadvertent testimony of the crowd: "He saved others; he can't save himself!" (Matthew 27:42). The words were shouted in defiance and ridicule, but the thief wondered, *What could they mean, "He saved others"?*

As the mob rehearsed some of the sayings and miracles of Jesus, he pondered their mockery and began to realize he just might be in the presence of a savior.

What is more, Pilate wrote what someone has called a "gospel tract" and had it nailed above the cross. It was customary to write the crime of the crucified man on a billboard put above the cross so passersby could see the reason for the execution. Pilate had written, "THIS IS THE KING OF THE JEWS" (Luke 23:38). Some objected. "Do not write 'The King of the Jews,' but rather, 'This man said, I am King of the Jews'" (John 19:21). But Pilate, in a rare burst of courage, would not change his mind. So there it hung.

When Jesus was paraded through the streets of Jerusalem, this plaque would have accompanied Him. Now on the cross, this thief might have read the words, or more likely, others read them aloud in mockery. At any rate, he now believed that Jesus was a king, for he pleaded, "Jesus, remember me when you come into your *kingdom*" (Luke 23:42, emphasis added). Incredibly, God birthed faith in this man's heart.

Think of it! He believed at a time when it appeared that Jesus was entirely helpless to save anyone; in fact, He Himself appeared to need saving! Jesus hung as a hapless victim, not a king. When you need saving, you do not turn to someone who is in the same predicament as you. When you need saving, you do not turn to someone who is dying in disgrace. Common sense tells us that a savior must rise above the fate of mortals.

What savior would wear a crown of thorns matted with blood? What savior would have His beard plucked out by the roots? Jesus' body was slumped, the nails having ripped His hands and feet. His chin rested on His chest, except when He gathered enough strength to lift His head that He might breathe. What a pathetic sight! And yet for all that, the thief believed!

A messiah who could be murdered by His enemies was not what the Jews had been looking for. Messianic speculation said that He was to rout the Romans who occupied the land and establish a kingdom. When Jesus explained to His disciples that He had to be crucified, they were dumbfounded. And on this day, even those who trusted Him were doubting. Just as the blood flowed from Christ's body, so faith flowed from the heart of His followers. Yet the thief believed!

This thief believed before darkness settled over the land; he believed before the earthquake and before the veil of the temple was torn in two. He believed without the evidence of the resurrection and the ascension. He believed without seeing Jesus walk on the water, feed the multitudes, or turn water into wine. Improbable as it was, he believed.

Arthur Pink challenges us to ask, "How can we explain the fact that this dying thief took a suffering, bleeding, crucified man for his God!"[3] The answer cannot be found by doing a psychological analysis of him. The answer is found in the undeserved mercy of God. The Holy Spirit was drawing this hoodlum's heart toward the Man on the middle cross. And he believed.

The thief's journey of faith began when he rebuked his partner in crime: "Do you not even fear God, seeing you are under the same condemnation? And we indeed justly" (Luke 23:40–41 NKJV). His awakened conscience told him that he should have feared God, for judgment was coming. He honestly admitted that he was suffering "justly"; that is, he was getting what he deserved. He did not justify himself nor make excuses. He could only hope that his partner on the other side would admit to his own sins too.

Struggling with each word, he turned and said to Jesus, "*Remember* me when you come into your kingdom" (Luke 23:42, emphasis added). He did not ask to be honored when Christ came into His kingdom; he asked only that he be remembered. He was an outcast from society, someone his friends and family would be most happy to forget. His request was modest—"*Remember* me"—but what an honor to be remembered by God.

His was a courageous faith. The crowd was mocking Jesus. The rabble-rousers were chanting insults: "If you are a king, where is your kingdom?" And again, "If you are a king, come down from the cross!"[4] This thief defied the common consensus. He turned away from the growing chorus of voices that would have led him astray. A friend of mine said that he would embrace Christ as Savior only if he were to move away from his family and friends. The thought of their rejection and ridicule was too much to bear; he could believe only in secret. No wonder we are told that hell is filled with "the fearful and unbelieving." This thief cared not about the opinion of others. He believed.

HIS AMAZING FUTURE

Jesus exceeded the repentant thief's expectations. "Truly, I say to you, today you will be with me in Paradise" (Luke 23:43).

The reunion would be *that very day*. The phrase "you will be *with me*" describes the personal fellowship they would enjoy together. The greatest blessing for the Christian is that God has called us "into the fellowship of his Son" (1 Corinthians 1:9). The previous night, Jesus made a similar promise to His close friends: "And if I go and prepare a place for you,

I will come again and will take you to myself, that where I am you may be also" (John 14:3). Incredibly, this thief received the same promise as the disciples! He was as safe in the arms of Jesus as he would have been if he had served the Lord from his youth.

Whether or not Jesus descended into hades, as the Apostles' Creed teaches, is debated by theologians. If He did, He was there but for a short time, for He promised the thief that they would be together that very day. Some folks, bless them, believe in "soul sleep," the notion that the soul sleeps unconsciously until the day of resurrection. But this doctrine is not taught in the Scriptures but rather is found in the writings of a so-called prophetess who has, on many counts, been found to be unreliable. This is not the place for fancy theories or wordplays. Jesus said, "*Today* you will be with me in Paradise."

Obviously, Jesus died before the thief did, and He was on hand to welcome him into the eternal dwelling place. Spurgeon wrote that this "man who was our Lord's last companion on earth" was His "first companion at the gates of paradise."[5] The thief was with Him in condemnation and hours later was with Him in salvation. If the dying Christ could give the thief a promise of eternal salvation, think of what the living Christ can do!

At the risk of being clearer than I would have to be, I point out the following facts about the thief's salvation:

- He did not make an intermediate stop in purgatory en route to paradise.
- He was not baptized.
- He did not receive last rites or Holy Communion.
- He did not ask Mary, who was standing at the foot of the cross, for help in approaching Jesus.

To make the promise more emphatic, Jesus prefaced it with the words "Truly, I say to you." This was a promise drawn on the bank of heaven, and it was as trustworthy as the Man who gave it. Hanging in apparent helplessness, Jesus still controlled the gate to paradise. He had power to make a promise to the repentant and to judge the guilty. Never did Jesus act more truly as a king than at that moment.

HIS FAITH IS TESTED

Let's put ourselves in the dying thief's predicament. He hears the promise from the lips of Jesus, but, later, at twelve noon, darkness spreads over the whole land. He hears his newly found Savior cry, "My God, my God, why have you forsaken me?" (Matthew 27:46). This is followed by an earthquake and rocks being split in two. "The curtain of the temple was torn in two, from top to bottom. And the earth shook, and the rocks were split" (v. 51).

As he sees the darkness and is jostled as the earth beneath him shifts; as he hears the cry of distress from the very One in whom he had come to trust, waves of doubt wash his faith away. Perhaps this Savior cannot save after all! How can He bring sinners into the presence of the very God who now has abandoned Him? How can He speak with authority about heaven when He apparently cannot control the chaos on earth?

Doubts or not, the promise of Jesus was still valid. Even if the thief's faith vanished in those last three horrific hours, his destiny was assured. Jesus had spoken, and that was all that mattered. "Whoever believes in the Son has eternal life; whoever does not obey the Son shall not see life, but the wrath of God remains on him" (John 3:36).

I've known Christians suffering from Alzheimer's disease who could no longer remember that they had trusted Christ as their Savior. Others, fully in charge of their mental faculties, have gone through intense emotional distress when death approached. A missionary who spent years sharing the gospel with others experienced a torturous death from cancer. His false hopes of recovery and broken dreams washed his faith away. He died believing he was abandoned by God. His last words were, "I feel trapped."

William Cowper, a poet who loved God and was converted to Christ at an early age, suffered from mental illness and during his bouts of depression believed he was damned. One evening he wrote:

> *God moves in a mysterious way*
> *His wonders to perform.*[6]

Yet, that very night, Cowper tried to commit suicide. And when he failed in his attempt, he believed he was as "damned as Judas." But those who knew him testified to his great love for God and the gospel. He had passionately believed in Christ, and, at the end of the day, that is all that mattered. The turbulence of his mental state did not nullify the promise of Jesus, and it is His promise that counts.

Let the thief languish; let him have misgivings; let him think that the One in whom he had put his faith was unable to keep His promise—it matters not. God has spoken. That day he will be with Jesus in paradise. And when he hears Jesus' final prayer, "Father, into your hands I commit my spirit" (Luke 23:46), no doubt his faith revives. The suffering is now tolerable, for this miserable day will soon come to an end.

This remarkable story carries some lessons for us.

TRANSFORMING LESSONS

Let us remember that both thieves prayed, but only one was saved. The other thief said, "If You are the Christ, save Yourself and us" (Luke 23:39 NKJV). The suffering man is thinking, *If Jesus was a king, why did He not exercise His kingship and save all three crucified that day?* This other thief wanted to extend his life on earth for a few more days or years. What if Jesus had answered this prayer and saved Himself and both of the others? He would have aborted the plan of God and would not have been able to save anyone else. This thief's problem was that he cared only about this life, not the next. "There was no remorse for his sins; only distress that he was suffering the consequences of them."[7] Jesus died so that the forgiven thief could be in paradise and so that you and I would be able to join Him in the future.

Jesus was numbered with the transgressors so that you and I could be numbered with the redeemed. Though personally sinless, He was counted as a transgressor by both God and man. He got what He didn't deserve, namely, our sin; and we got what we didn't deserve, namely, His righteousness. "For our sake he made him to be sin who knew no sin, so that in him we might become the righteousness of God" (2 Corinthians 5:21).

Both thieves had an equal opportunity. Both heard the words of Jesus, "Father, forgive them." Both knew that Jesus was ridiculed for claiming that He was the King of the Jews. Both heard the witness of Jesus' enemies, "He saved others; let him save himself, if he is the Christ of God, his Chosen One!" (Luke 23:35). And yet, these thieves will be apart forever, each in his own separate destiny. Even as you read these words, one is in the presence of Jesus, the other in a place of isolation, grief, and horror. What separated them was not the degree of their wickedness nor their distance from Christ; they are separated because one called on Christ for help and the other derided Him.

These thieves represent the entire human race. Ultimately, the world is not divided geographically, racially, or economically. Nor can we draw a line separating the relatively good people from the relatively bad ones. All races, nations, and cultures are divided by the cross. On one side are those individuals who believe, and on the other are those who choose to justify themselves, determined to stand before God on their own record. Heaven and hell are not places far away, but near us. Everything depends on what we do with Jesus.

Finally, my dear reader, today is the day to believe on Christ. Some people see the thief as an example of a "deathbed conversion," and I've met people who believe that someday, they too will believe just before they die. But few—very few—are saved in the last few hours or days of their lives on earth. One of the Puritans, commenting on the thief's deathbed conversion, perceptively said, "There is one such case recorded that none need despair, but only one that none might presume."

Warren Wiersbe points out that this man was not saved at his last opportunity, but at his *first* opportunity. He was not there when Jesus turned water into wine; he was not there when Jesus stilled the storm or fed the multitude; he did not hear the Sermon on the Mount or Christ's words to the paralytic, "Your sins are forgiven." This was his first opportunity to believe on Christ.

There are two powerful reasons we should not delay in accepting Christ as our personal sin bearer. For one thing, we do not know the time of our death. Not everyone has a warning; not everyone dies of a terminal illness or remains conscious after a car accident. Millions die unexpectedly, without so much as a minute to think about their relationship with God. Second, most people who refuse the gospel when they are healthy reject it when it is time to die. The older we get, our hearts are either drawn closer to Christ or impelled to move away from Him. Neutrality is impossible.

The unrepentant thief proves the point: see him there on the cross hanging in unimaginable agony. He has the sure knowledge that he is about to die; his friend has helped him become aware of his great sins. And yet, incredibly, he ridicules Jesus with his dying breath! Like most people, he died just as he lived. No wonder the writer of Hebrews asked, "How shall we escape if we neglect such a great salvation?" (Hebrews 2:3). The answer, of course, is that there is no escape.

In contrast, the repentant thief gives us the hope we all seek. Though his sins were many, he is a witness to God's undeserved grace. He is proof that one act of faith can save even the worst of sinners. In fact, the issue is not the greatness of our sin but our willingness to believe that determines our destiny.

William Cowper, though plagued with doubts, understood that if the thief could be saved, we all can be. He wrote a song titled "There Is a Fountain Filled with Blood." One of my favorite stanzas reads:

> *The dying thief rejoiced to see*
> *That fountain in his day;*
> *And there may I, though vile as he,*
> *Wash all my sins away.*[8]

The thief's forgiveness reminds us that there is more grace in God's heart than sin in our past. We, like he, can also receive a welcome in the life beyond if we transfer our trust to the One who holds the key to the gates of paradise.

CHAPTER 3

A CRY OF
COMPASSION

"Woman, here is your son . . .Here is your mother."
—JOHN 19:26–27 NIV

Depend upon it, Sir, when a man knows he is to be hanged in a fortnight," wrote Samuel Johnson, "it concentrates his mind wonderfully."[1] If ever there was a moment when we would expect a man to think only of himself, it is at the hour of his death. The awareness that eternity awaits rids the mind of all but the most anxious thoughts. And if the throes of death are especially painful, we would expect the sufferer to focus exclusively on his own immediate needs.

Jesus, hanging on the cross, thought of others.

Before the Father's presence was obscured and darkness spread throughout the land, Jesus made provision for

His mother. William Barclay writes, "There is something infinitely moving in the fact that Jesus in the agony of the cross, in the moment when the salvation of the world hung in the balance, thought of the loneliness of his mother in the days when he was taken away."[2] He remained a faithful firstborn Son until the end.

We can assume that Joseph, the legal father of Jesus, had long since died. The last time he is mentioned is when Jesus stayed behind in Jerusalem when He was twelve years old. His parents returned only to find Him in the temple discussing doctrinal matters with the teacher of the law (Luke 2:46). With this story, Joseph passes from the scene, though Mary is mentioned many times throughout Jesus' public ministry. As the eldest son in a single parent home, Jesus must provide for her.

As Jesus began speaking, the soldiers were casting lots for His undergarment. "They said to one another, 'let us not tear it, but cast lots for it to see whose it shall be'" (John 19:24). Jewish men usually wore five pieces of clothing. When we read that the soldiers "divided them into four parts . . . also his tunic. But the tunic was seamless " (v. 23), it does not mean that they tore the clothes apart but that they had divided up the four pieces. But they had to decide who would get the fifth garment, the seamless undergarment. Usually this tunic was given to the son by his mother. Legend says that Mary gave Jesus this tunic when He left home. Perhaps the legend is true.

Charles Swindoll points out that there seems to be a connection between what the soldiers were doing and the words of Jesus. Immediately after we are told that the soldiers were casting lots for His tunic, we read, "Standing by the cross of Jesus were his mother" (John 19:25). Then follow the words of Jesus to Mary and to John.

Swindoll writes, "Why now? She's been there all along, watching and weeping. Why hasn't He acknowledged or spoken to her? Could it be because of the seamless tunic? I think so. His outer garments were insignificant.... But when they touched the tunic, they touched something very near to His heart—the garment made for Him by His mother."[3] Swindoll's point is that when the soldiers began haggling over the tunic, it was then that Jesus looked at His mother. The gracious words that now came from His lips were filled with love, pity, and nostalgia.

We've learned that John returned to stand at the foot of the cross to watch his Master suffer and die. Though in unutterable pain, Jesus turned to him and to His own mother, Mary, who was standing nearby with three other women. No longer would He be able to care for her, for the nature of their relationship would be changed forever. We listen carefully to every word.

"Woman, here is your son" (John 19:26 NIV).

He spoke with His chin resting on His chest, eyes riveted to the ground. Though He also was her Son, He was not referring to Himself; this time He uses the word *son* to refer to John, "the disciple whom Jesus loved" (John 13:23 NIV). She would have to "adopt" John as if he were her very own. As best he could, John would fill the aching void Jesus' death would bring. Mary was losing one Son but gaining another.

Scarcely had He uttered those words when another groan came from His parched lips. He strained to be heard, and now He tried to glance in John's direction.

"Here is your mother" (John 19:27 NIV).

John was designated to take care of Mary as if she were his own mother.

A MOTHER'S LOVE

For a moment, let's put ourselves in the shoes of Mary, chosen to bear the Son of God. After the angel visited her, she was both excited and apprehensive; she was honored but humbled. With faithful obedience she replied to Gabriel, "Let it be to me according to your word" (Luke 1:38). After Jesus was born, she and Joseph took the baby Jesus into the temple, and the aged Simeon predicted that a sword would pass through her own heart (Luke 2:35). Of course, at the time, she could not have anticipated what all this would mean. She could not have predicted the birth in the manger, the years of conflict, and then the death that would tear her heart apart. Simeon was, oh, so right. If she was to have a Son, she was also to have a sword. Great privileges bring great sorrows.

The first time the sword pierced her heart was when innocent babies were massacred near Bethlehem because of Herod's fear of the Messiah (Matthew 2:16–18). The small family fled to Egypt, but surely she knew that it was because of her Son that soldiers entered the houses to murder the infant sons in full view of their families. The whole region wept, and Mary and her Son were the cause of it all.

The sword struck again when she and her family listened to the whispers that implied that her Son was conceived in shame. She overheard the ridicule, the insults, and the threats. She knew that people tried to push her Son over a cliff in Nazareth; she knew that He was sought like the hawk seeks the mouse. And because she knew that He was innocent—perfect in all respects—the injustice of it all weighed upon her soul.

Think of what it must have been like to have Jesus grow up in an ordinary, imperfect Jewish home! We can only imagine the strain on the family relationships. The other children no doubt always felt inferior to their older brother, who never disobeyed, never lied, and, in short, never sinned. They soon learned that they could not blame Him for their misdeeds! Mary knew His perfections but now had to endure the misunderstandings, mockings, and scorn heaped upon Him. She knew that her Son was accomplishing a heavenly mission.

Finally, now at the cross, the sword divided Mary's heart, piercing her to the depths. When at last the soldier pierced the side of her Son, it felt as if the sword had already sliced the heart of this mother. She who had planted kisses on the brow of that little child now saw that brow crowned with thorns. She who had held those little hands as He learned to walk now saw those hands pierced with nails. She who had cradled Him in her arms now saw Him writhing alone on the garbage dump of Jerusalem. She who loved Him at birth came to love Him even more in death. As Pink put it, "Never such bliss at a human birth, never such sorrow at an inhuman death."[4]

She knew that He had the power to come down from the cross; she knew about the legions of angels at His disposal. But when He said, "Dear woman, here is your son," and nodded toward John, she understood that He was preparing her for His death. The earthly ties were over, and a new heavenly relationship was about to begin. He would no longer be her Son but her Savior.

Mary suffers in unbroken silence. She sees the crown of thorns but cannot remove it; she sees the nails but is not allowed to pull them out; she sees the lacerations but is not able to soothe her Son's pain with salve; she hears the mockery but is not able to quiet the crowd. It was always dangerous to be associated with a man who was believed by the Romans to be worthy of crucifixion. But she stood by His side, for though He was derided as a criminal, she knew better.

She stands by the cross; she does not swoon, she does not crouch, she does not run; she stands and sees it all. This was the hour of which Jesus had spoken; the hour from which there could be no escape. As His mother, she could only stand by, touched by His intolerable grief. She is the woman whom artists draw with a lily in hand, but someone has suggested that the white lily is stained with the red blood of a broken heart. Yes, the sword had struck its most sensitive target.

She would have gladly traded places with Him, but she could not help Him bring redemption. She might have been able to save Him if she had gone to the authorities and argued that what He said was not true and that He should be acquitted by reason of insanity. Or, more tempting, she could have simply pled for mercy. But she will not interfere with the mystery of the divine will.

Though she could not understand, she could love.

Wonderful mother that she was, she nevertheless took her place with the other sinners at the foot of the cross. She was not there to aid in purchasing redemption, but she herself was being redeemed by her Son. In the lovely poem we call the Magnificat, composed after she discovered she was pregnant, she said, "My soul magnifies the Lord, and my spirit rejoices in God *my Savior*" (Luke 1:46–47, emphasis added). She too needed the forgiveness her Son was now purchasing.

A SON'S EXAMPLE

Jesus was mindful of how much pain He had caused His dear mother. He called her "Woman," just as He did at the wedding in Canaan. He was not disrespectful, but she must remember that He was a heavenly Son and she an earthly mother. In fact, nowhere is it recorded that He called her "Mother." John referred to Mary as the mother of Jesus, but Jesus Himself never used the word, perhaps to help us remember that she was only the human vessel through whom He came into the world.

Why did Jesus not commit His mother to His half brothers, the children Mary bore Joseph after the miraculous virgin birth? (They are named in Matthew 13:55.) For one thing, they were not in Jerusalem but in the area of Galilee. For another, we know that when they grew up, they could not admit to themselves that their older brother was, in fact, the Messiah. Even late in His ministry we read, "For not even his brothers believed in him" (John 7:5). Thankfully, the events of the crucifixion and resurrection changed their minds, for they were among those who met in the upper room when the Holy Spirit came at Pentecost (Acts 1:14). So at this point, He committed her to a new "son," John.

A DISCIPLE'S RESPONSIBILITY

When Jesus was taken into custody, we read, "Then all the disciples left him and fled" (Matthew 26:56). We would think that their love for Him would have weathered any storm, including death. Peter thought so (v. 35). But at the crunch time, they ran because they were offended at Him, just as He predicted (v. 31 KJV). That word *offended* means scandalized; to put it plainly, they deserted Him because they were ashamed of Him.

I've often reflected on the words of Satan to God, "All that a man has he will give for his life" (Job 2:4). Scan the pages of history and you will be surprised at how much greater value we place on our physical lives than we do on our principles or even our souls. Many people have deep convictions but not deep enough to suffer for their cause. Often it takes very little to have our faith overturned, just as Peter discovered.

But the failure of the disciples was also a matter of divine providence. Isaiah predicted that the Messiah would tread "the winepress alone" (Isaiah 63:3). Arthur Pink wrote, "Christ must not have the least relief or comfort from any creature . . . that He might be left alone to grapple with the wrath of God and man."[5] When John returned, he learned that when you come to the cross, you are given a new responsibility.

"No one at work knows that I'm a Christian," a businessman said to me. Then he added, "I like it that way because then I'm not put on a pedestal; I don't have to live up to this unreal standard." He preferred to live far from the cross, unnoticed among the masses who frequent the religious smorgasbords of our day. I encouraged him to return to the cross that he claims redeemed him. I urged him to come with his guilt and fears. I reminded him of the words of Jesus, "For whoever is ashamed of me and of my words in this adulterous and sinful generation, of him will the Son of Man also be ashamed when he comes in the glory of his Father with the holy angels" (Mark 8:38). This carnal man must return to the cross to receive his assignment. No one can come to the cross without seeing it as a place of selfless devotion. We come to the cross to die to our own plans and ambitions and accept the mantel given to us by the One who hung there for us.

Jesus did not rebuke John for having left, but rather, when he returned he was given a glorious honor. It was fitting that John should be given the privilege of caring for Mary, since he had understood the love of Christ better than all the other apostles. Three days later, Peter and John were the first to run to the sepulcher; Peter went in and noticed the orderly arrangement of the grave clothes. Then John entered, and we read, "He saw and believed" (John 20:8); that is, he knew that Jesus was raised from the dead.

What did the disciples do with this exciting news? They returned to their own homes (John 20:10). That means that John hurried home to tell Mary that her Son had risen from the dead. Years later, Jesus would reveal to John the Apocalypse (the book of Revelation). There he would see the Lord Jesus as the Sovereign Lord. What reflections must have passed through his mind as he remembered his fellowship with Jesus on earth and the joy of caring for His mother!

If it is true that God created in order that He might redeem, Jesus was now doing the work for which the world was made. Here on the center cross the purpose of the ages would be consummated. This was the hub into which the spokes of God's purposes would come together in a beautiful display of divine attributes. Both God's love and justice were put on display for all to see. Yet at this moment, Jesus did not overlook His earthly family obligations.

LIVING NEAR THE CROSS

If we had been there, how close would we have stood to the cross? Nearby or at a comfortable distance? Would we have been intimidated by the mob, or would we have gladly let the angry rabble-rousers know that we were followers of the Man hanging on the middle cross? Would we stand nearby even if the cross cost us as much as it cost Christ?

At the cross, we, like John, are asked to take Christ's place in the world. When Christ prayed the night before, He said, "As you sent me into the world, so I have sent them into the world" (John 17:18). Earlier, He taught His disciples, "If anyone comes to me and does not hate his own father and mother and wife and children and brothers and sisters, yes, even his own life, he cannot be my disciple. *Whoever who does not bear his own cross and come after me cannot be my disciple*" (Luke 14:26–27, emphasis added).

Would you have taken care of Mary if Jesus had asked? "Of course," you say, but how can we know for sure? We are given the same opportunity every day. When Jesus was interrupted by a man who wanted to tell Him that His mother and brothers were looking for Him, Jesus made an astounding statement. "'Who are my mother and my brothers?' And looking about at those who sat around him, he said, 'Here are my mother and my brothers! For whoever does the will of God, he is my brother and sister and mother'" (Mark 3:33–35).

We are His brothers, sisters, and mothers! Widows need someone else's son to take care of them. Single mothers need surrogate fathers for their children. The ill and infirm need to be visited and cared for with the same spirit by which Christ would serve them. "Truly, I say to you, as you did it to one of the least of these my brothers,, you did it to me" (Matthew 25:40). Our own parents need the same tender care we would afford to Mary. We are His body, His hands, His feet.

Some time ago I read a story about a woman whose husband left her for another woman. When the divorce was final, the errant husband remarried and had several children by his new wife. When he fell ill with cancer, he knew that his second wife would be incapable of taking care of his children. Knowing the deep compassion of his first wife, he requested that she adopt his children and rear them as if they were her own.

Incredibly, she accepted the challenge. When asked how

she could lovingly rear the children of her adulterous husband, she replied, "God's love gave me the grace to forgive and accept his children as my own."

I think I hear Jesus saying, "Woman, here are your children," and again, "Children, behold your mother." The groans of Christ from the cross must reach the ears of all who minister in this age of the fractured family. And many have discovered that spiritual bonds are even stronger than natural bonds in forming relationships. Sacrificial compassion is, after all, an unmistakable sign of the presence of Christ. Let us hear Him as He says to us, "Take my place until I come."

How glibly we sing:

> *Jesus, keep me near the cross,*
> *There a precious fountain*
> *Free to all—a healing stream,*
> *Flows from Calvary's mountain.*[6]

Salome, the mother of John and James, was standing at the cross that day (she is referred to in John 19:25 as Mary's sister). She was the one who had asked that her sons, James and John, have the privilege of ruling in the coming kingdom. That day she learned that there can be no selfishness at the foot of the cross. As Bonhoeffer wrote,

> When Christ calls a man, he bids him come and die. It may be a death like that of the first disciples who had to leave home and follow him, or it may be a death like Luther's, who had to leave the monastery and go out into the world. But it is the same death every time—death in Jesus Christ, the death of the old man at his call. . . . Only the man who is dead to his own will can follow Christ.[7]

The cross crushes all self-aggrandizement. Standing there with bowed heads, we have but one question: How can I be Your hands and feet in the world?

What a contrast outside the city of Jerusalem that day! On the one hand, redemption is being purchased for those God would redeem; on the other hand, the soldiers mark time by playing their tired games, waiting for the ordeal to be over. Those who love Jesus are in grieving despair; those who hate Him are in a mood of spiteful rejoicing. Heaven hovers over the cross, waiting for the payment of our sin to be made. But hell is there too, with its cruelty, indifference, and darkness.

Like the soldiers, some even today gamble their lives away in the shadow of the cross. They know of Jesus; some have been taught about Him in fine homes or evangelical churches. But it is not proximity to the cross that makes us believers. Sometimes those who have been closest to Christ have rejected Him with the most ardent determination.

Let us take our place with those who bow humbly to accept the responsibility that the cross places on each of us. "Far be if from me to boast except in the cross of our Lord Jesus Christ, by which the world has been crucified to me, and I to the world" (Galatians 6:14).

CHAPTER 4

A CRY OF ANGUISH

"My God, my God, why have you forsaken me?"
—MATTHEW 27:46

Only at the cross can we see the love of God without ambiguity. Here is His farthest reach, His most ambitious rescue effort. God personally came to our side of the chasm, willing to suffer for us and with us. At Golgotha His love burst upon the world with unmistakable clarity and brilliance. Here at last we have reason to believe that there was a genuine meeting between God and man.

At the cross, God's inflexible holiness and boundless love collided, and with a cry of anguish, we were redeemed. Here is sin with all of its horror and grace, with all of its wonder. The first three cries from the cross were uttered in daylight.

71

But now nature shrouded the suffering of its Creator with darkness. This cry of dereliction, as it is called, was appropriately the middle of the seven sayings, the one that leads us into the mystery of our suffering God.

"My God, my God, why have you forsaken me?" (Matthew 27:46; Mark 15:34).

Before we meditate on these words, we must take a moment to make sure that we do not misunderstand the relationship between the Father and the Son. Because we are going to speak about God the Son offering a sacrifice to God the Father, we might give the impression that a benevolent Son persuaded a reluctant Father to do something about the plight of humanity and He grudgingly agreed.

Not so.

The Scriptures do say that Christ was "stricken, smitten by God, and afflicted" (Isaiah 53:4), and again, "Yet it was the will of the LORD to crush him; he has put him to grief" (v. 10), but the image of an angry God exacting every ounce of payment from a submissive Christ can distort our understanding of the Almighty. If we are not careful, we can think of the Son as loving and the Father as cruel and harsh.

Such a notion flounders in the face of God's love. Indeed, the saving work of Christ originated in the heart of the Father. The best-known verse in the Bible teaches that "God so loved the world" (John 3:16). And Zechariah said that Christ came "because of the tender mercy of our God" (Luke 1:78). Salvation came to us because our Father is a redeeming God who loves us. The Father and the Son took the initiative of redemption together.

John Stott wrote:

> We must not, then, speak of God punishing Jesus or of
> Jesus persuading God, for to do so is to set them over
> against each other as if they acted independently of each
> other or were even in conflict with each other. . . . The
> Father did not lay on the Son an ordeal he was reluctant
> to bear, nor did the Son extract from the Father a salva-
> tion he was reluctant to bestow.[1]

Christ did not die to make the Father loving, for He loved
us from the foundation of the world. The will of the Father
and the will of the Son coincided in the perfect self-sacrifice
of love. If the Father turned away from the Son at the cross,
it was because they agreed it must be so to purchase our redemption. It was a horrid necessity.

Nor should we misrepresent the Trinity as we approach
this sacred cry. When Jesus cried, "My God, my God, why
have you forsaken me?" we should not think that the Father
and the Son became separated in their "being" or "essence."
In other words, when the Father forsook the Son, the Trinity
did not divide in two. This was a break in fellowship, not a
breach of the fundamental unity of the Father and the Son.

Now we again approach the cross and hear this cry of
Jesus. Here all of the forces of the universe converge: *Man*
did his work by killing the Son of God and revealing the evil
of his heart; *Satan* did his work by bruising the seed of the
woman and displaying his foolish hostility; *Jesus* did a work,
for He died, "the just for the unjust, that he might bring us
to God" (1 Peter 3:18 KJV); and, finally, *God* did a work by
exhibiting His justice and love when His wrath was poured
out on His Son.[2]

If God is to bless us, He must turn His back upon Himself. Surely, we must approach the cross with wonder.

THE WONDER OF THE DARKNESS

According to Jewish custom, a new day began at 6:00 in the morning. So when we read that Jesus was crucified at the third hour, we understand this to be at 9:00 a.m. So for three hours He hung in the morning sunlight; but then at the sixth hour, that is, at midday, darkness spread over the land. "From the sixth hour there was darkness over all the land until the ninth hour" (Matthew 27:45). At high noon, the world became dark. There had been three hours of light, but now there would be three hours of darkness. This was not an eclipse; the sun was obscured by a supernatural act of God.

Why night, at noon?

Darkness is always associated with the judgment of God for great sin. Here we see the judgment of God against the evil men who treated His Son with cruel contempt; and, in a profound sense, we stand condemned with them, for it was our sins that put Jesus on the cross. Should we ever love sin, we would love the very evil that caused nails to be driven through our Savior's hands and feet. Just as we would abhor the knife that was used to murder a child, so we should abhor the sin that caused Jesus to die. Darkness came because of the collective guilt of us all.

But there is another reason for the darkness. It represents the judgment of the Father against His Son. In those hours of darkness, Jesus became legally guilty of our sin, and for that He was judged. Think of it: legally guilty of genocide, child abuse, alcoholism, murder, adultery, homosexual activity, greed, and the like. How appropriate that when the Sinless One was "made sin for us," the event was veiled from human eyes.

Recall that, in Egypt, the last plague before the Passover was a "darkness that can be felt" (Exodus 10:21 NIV). Now, just before this Passover lamb was slain, darkness covered the world like a blanket. Only when He died did light return.

> *Well might the sun in darkness hide,*
> *And shut his glories in,*
> *When Christ, the Great Maker, died*
> *For man, the creature's sin.*[3]

Now we probe even further into the relationship between Father and Son.

THE WONDER OF THE QUESTION

"*My God, my God,* why have you forsaken me?"

What a contrast with His previous experience with the Father!

In the garden of Gethsemane, Jesus has a God who strengthens Him; on the cross, He has a God who turns away from Him. In Gethsemane, He can call twelve legions of angels who would have been quick to deliver Him; on the cross, He cries to God, who refuses deliverance. Previously, He said the Father has not left Him alone; now, the Father has turned His face. In Gethsemane, the Son was tempted to forsake the Father; on the cross, the Father forsook the Son.[4]

Let us analyze the question.

Only here, in the Gospel record, does Jesus address His Father as "God." This change of address signified the break in fellowship between Father and Son. At this moment, the Father did not seem to be acting like a Father. The suffering of the Son was intolerable enough, but to endure it without the Father's presence magnified the horror.

This cry is so difficult for us to accept that some have

suggested that the Father did not really forsake the Son, but Jesus only *felt* forsaken. But we must give the words their plain meaning. Calvin was right in saying that Christ's soul had also to feel the full effects of judgment. "If Christ had died only a bodily death, it would have been ineffectual. . . . Unless his soul had shared in the punishment, he would have been the redeemer of bodies alone." In consequence, "he paid a greater and more excellent price in suffering in his soul the terrible torments of a condemned and forsaken man." Make no mistake: This was a real abandonment by the Father.

Forsaken. It is a powerful word. A man forsaken by his friends. A wife forsaken by her husband. A creature forsaken by his creator. A son forsaken by his father. This Son had been the object of the Father's love from all eternity; the Father's presence was His only delight. The hiding of His Father's face was the most bitter sip of the cup of sorrow He chose to drink.

But did He suffer only as man, or did He suffer as God? Was the divine nature passive while the Father was accepting the payment that was being made on that dark day in Jerusalem?

Dennis Ngien has argued that a God who cannot suffer is a God who cannot love. If God cannot feel the pain of His people, we might be tempted to say that God is indifferent to our plight. "God suffers," wrote Dennis Ngien, "because God wills to love."[5]

Perhaps Bonhoeffer was right when he wrote from prison, "Only the suffering God can help [us]."[6]

If only the humanity of Christ suffered at the cross, then there was no real incarnation. Indeed, it might lead to the conclusion that only a man died on the cross, not the God-man. He could not suffer as man without His divine nature suffering too. Nor can I believe that the Father remained passive and unmoved. As parents, we know that if we watched our son die he would not be the only one suffering. Even so, our heavenly Father felt the pain of His beloved Son. God had to turn His back upon Himself, that He might pay the penalty for our sin.

Keep in mind that the Father was not forced to suffer because of circumstances beyond His control. God *chose* to suffer. He *chose* to redeem humanity through the suffering of His Son. The Father chose to be accepted by some people and rejected by others. He suffered because He willed it so. He had before Him an indefinite number of possible worlds—worlds in which there was no fall, no sin, no need of redemption. Yet He chose this plan with its injustice and pain. We are invited to believe that, looked at from eternity, this plan was best.

If we as redeemed sinners think it terrifying to be forsaken by God, think of the grief of the Son, who was with the Father from all eternity; think of Him being forsaken! His holiness was in contact with impurity of every kind. And yet, even in this cry, there is hope and trust. He says, "*My God, my God* . . ." He still called God "*My* God"; the Father still belonged to Him. The sweet communion was gone, but the Son had the full knowledge that the Father's presence would return. The withdrawal of the Father's presence did not mean the withdrawal of His love. At the end of the dark tunnel was light; in a few hours He would say, "Father, into your hands I commit my spirit" (Luke 23:46).

"This was a cry of distress but not of distrust," wrote Pink. "God had withdrawn from Him, but mark how His soul still cleaves to God."[7] The anguish cannot be captured in words. No wonder when Luther contemplated this text, he agonized over the mystery and exclaimed, "God forsaking God, no man can understand that!"

Yes, the darkness reminds us of the horror and the mystery. A mystery no man can understand.

THE WONDER OF THE SILENCE

"My God, my God, why have you *forsaken* me?"

The cry rings out to a silent heaven.

Two thousand years before this, Abraham was asked to kill his son Isaac on an altar at the top of Moriah, but just as his knife was raised to the sky, Jehovah intervened. "Do not lay your hand on the boy or do anything to him, for now I know that you fear God, seeing you have not withheld your son, your only son, from me" (Genesis 22:12). So Isaac's life was spared. But the voice that called out on Moriah is now silent at Calvary.

So why *was* the Son forsaken by the Father?

The angels, no doubt, searched for an answer, for they have a deep interest in those matters that pertain to our salvation (1 Peter 1:12). The Pharisees standing at a distance from the cross would not have been able to give an answer. The priests would not understand; nor would the Roman soldiers. Just so today, many people do not understand why God would forsake anyone, especially the Son whom He dearly loves.

That the sum of all perfection should be forsaken by the Father; that the One in whom is all the fullness of the Godhead should not see the Father's face—for this there must be a grand reason. And we find the reason in Psalm 22. "My God, my God, why have you forsaken me? Why are you so far from saving me, from the words of my groaning? O my

God, I cry by day, but you do not answer, and by night, but I find no rest. *Yet you are holy, enthroned on the praises of Israel"* (Psalm 22:1–3, emphasis added).

The Father forsook the Son because His holiness required it. The prophet Nahum asked a question that needed to be answered: "Who can stand before his indignation? Who can endure the heat of his anger? His wrath is poured out like fire, and the rocks are broken into pieces by him" (Nahum 1:6). Only Jesus could withstand the indignation of the Father against sin; only Jesus could take the wrath we so richly deserved.

Keep in mind that Jesus was regarded by His enemies as a great sinner, but the Father regarded Him as doubly so. Or, more accurately, the Father regarded Him as the One who bore upon His shoulders the sin of many; thus He was reckoned as One guilty of heinous crimes. He was cursed in our place, that we might be set free. "Christ redeemed us from the curse of the law by becoming a curse for us—for it is written, 'Cursed is everyone who is hanged on a tree'" (Galatians 3:13). Visualize Jesus covered with that which is evil; visualize your sin laid upon His chest.

Might it not be (we can only speculate) that if Jesus died to deliver from an infinite hell all those who would believe on Him—might it not be that His suffering on the cross was, in some sense, "infinite"? Surely He endured the suffering of hell, for hell is darkness, abandonment, and being forsaken by God. If so, the horror of what He experienced is beyond us.

Let us suppose that Jesus was just a man; a perfect man but nothing more. He could only make a sacrifice for one other person. But Jesus was a sacrifice for many people, so He had to compress an eternity of hell into three hours. As best we can, we must grasp that this was infinite suffering for the infinite Son of God. There was no way to transfer sin without transferring its penalty. To put it plainly, He was receiving what was due us. The wrath of the Father burned toward the Son once the reckoning was made. Indescribable sin was in contact with infinite holiness and infinite justice.

Now we can better understand why it was midnight at midday. The physical darkness was symbolic of Christ's separation from the Father, who is Light. Just as the wicked are thrown into "outer darkness," so the Son bore the darkness of our hell. Stott wrote, "Our sins blotted out the sunshine of his Father's face."[8] Look at these hours on the cross and you are looking into hell: darkness, loneliness, and abandonment by God. This explains the cup He would have preferred not to drink. Throughout His lifetime He suffered at the hands of men; at specified times He suffered at the hands of Satan. But now He suffered at the hands of God.

He was abandoned to outer darkness that we might walk in the light.

THE WONDER OF
THE HUMAN HEART

Once more let us recreate the scene at Golgotha. The jeering crowd became plaintive and restless during the three hours of darkness. We might expect that they would be stricken with fear, anxiously wondering whether daylight would ever return. Perhaps this was the Son of God after all.

What was their response? "Some of bystanders, hearing it, said, 'This man is calling Elijah'" (Matthew 27:47). One man, as an expression of sympathy, got a sponge, filled it with wine and vinegar, put it on a reed, and offered it to Him. But as for the rest, they sarcastically said, "Wait, let us see whether Elijah will come to save him" (v. 49). I doubt that they misunderstood His words. Matthew actually records the Aramaic version of Jesus' words, which would have been known to the people milling about the cross. The comment about Elijah was made in derision.

The Jews present should have known that the cry, "My God," was a quotation from Psalm 22:1. The rest of this psalm describes in detail the ordeal of crucifixion. The Jews did not use crucifixion but stoned those deemed worthy of capital punishment. Yet as further proof of the trustworthiness of Scripture, crucifixion and not stoning is predicted as the means by which the Messiah would die.

I ask, "What would it have taken for these people to come to their senses and accept Jesus as the Son of God?" But then I must ask, "What will it take for people I know to come to their senses about Christ?" Today, as then, men and women harden their hearts against what seems most obvious to those who are open to the truth. The credentials of Christ can be seen by all who care to see. The more light that is given, the harder the human heart must become to reject it.

TRANSFORMING LESSONS

We dare not leave this heartfelt cry from our Savior's lips without savoring its implications for our understanding and worship.

The first purpose of the cross was not for us, but for God. Yes, Jesus shed His blood for us, but it is even more true to say that He shed His blood for the Father. When the blood was sprinkled on the doorposts of the houses in Egypt, it was put there for the benefit of the families, but it was also put there for God. Jehovah said, "When I see the blood, I will pass over you" (Exodus 12:13). Whether the members of the family had committed great sins or lesser ones, it mattered not; when the Angel of Death saw the blood, the house was exempt from judgment.

Christ's death was a "sacrifice to God for a sweetsmelling savour" (Ephesians 5:2 KJV). Paul says that Christ died to demonstrate God's righteousness (Romans 3:25). God had fellowship with Old Testament saints, though there had not been a final reckoning of their sin. It might appear as if He had lowered His standards, overlooking their transgressions. So Jesus had to die to demonstrate that God is just. He could not overlook the sins of even His closest friends (such as Abraham). Thus the suffering of the Son was planned by the Father. As John Piper wrote, "Never before or since has there been such suffering, because, in all its dreadful severity, it was a suffering by design. It was planned by God the Father and embraced by the Son."[9]

There is a story about a man who was brought before a judge for speeding. The fine was assessed at a hundred dollars, but the man had no money to pay. In sheer sympathy the judge did what he did not have to do. He left the bench, laid aside his robe, stood by the defendant, took out a hundred-dollar bill and laid it on the table. Then he returned to put on his robe, walked back up the stairs to his desk, leaned over, took the one hundred-dollar bill he had laid down, and said to the defendant, "Thank you. You may go free." Just so, God the Son made a payment to God the Father for those who would accept the gift of eternal life.

I'm told that in an Italian church there is a picture of the crucifixion with a vast shadowy figure behind the portrait of Christ. The nail that pierces the hand of Jesus goes through the hand of God. The spear thrust into the side of Jesus goes through into God's. Luther said that if it is not true that God died for us, but only a man died, then we are lost.

In one of my favorite hymns, Charles Wesley wrote words that cannot be excelled for their understanding of the cross and breadth of theology:

> *And can it be that I should gain*
> *An interest in the Saviour's blood?*
> *Died He for me, who caused His pain?*
> *For me, who Him to death pursued?*
> *Amazing love! how can it be*
> *That Thou, my God, shouldst die for me?*[10]

That Thou, my God, shouldst die for me! Of course, God cannot die, if by death we mean some form of annihilation. But if death is defined as separation (for us the separation of the spirit and the body), then God died in the sense that the Son was separated from the Father. "God, dying for man," wrote P. T. Forsyth, "I am not afraid of the phrase; I cannot do without it. God dying for men; and for such men—hostile, malignantly hostile men." Forsyth continued: "[God] must either inflict punishment or assume it. And he chose the latter course."[11]

Let us remember that He was forsaken by God that we might be accepted by Him. Let us hold to this promise: "Never will I leave you; never will I forsake you" (Hebrews 13:5 NIV). Paul assured us that nothing shall separate us from the love of Christ (Romans 8:35–39).

Jesus went through darkness that we might have light. He was cursed that we might be blessed. He was condemned that we might be able to say, "There is therefore now no condemnation for those who are in Christ Jesus" (Romans 8:1).

He suffered hell for us so that we can enjoy heaven with Him. "He entered the awful Darkness," wrote Pink, "that I might walk in the Light; He drank the cup of woe that I might drink the cup of joy; He was forsaken that I might be forgiven!"[12] Sin, like a loathsome serpent, clung to Him, but He bore the sting for us. We can hide behind the wall of His grace and know that we are safe from wrath.

"Without the cross," wrote Spurgeon, "there would have been a wound for which there was no ointment, a pain for which there was no balm."[13] Sin always exacts a payment. Either Jesus bears our sin, or we do. If the Father turned His face away from His beloved Son when He was regarded as a sinner, we can be sure that the Father will turn away from every sinner who stands before the Judgment Bar on his own merits. We are either saved by His rejection, or we must bear our own rejection for all of eternity. If those who are in hell should cry, "Why have You forsaken me?" heaven shall remain silent, for they receive the just recompense for their deeds.

Paul described the future horrid experience of those who do not find shelter beneath the work of Jesus on the cross: "They will suffer the punishment of eternal destruction, away from the presence of the Lord and from the glory of his might" (2 Thessalonians 1:9). Try to visualize eternal separation from Him who is the fount of all beauty and goodness, the One who is the source of life and love. Christ will say, "I never knew you. Away from me, you evildoers!" (Matthew 7:23 NIV).

A man who had no regard for God lay dying in a small cabin. As his final breaths approached, he asked his daughter to blow out the candle that was on the table. She said, "No, Daddy, you can't die in the dark." But he replied, "Yes, I will die in the dark." He died as he had lived. Live in darkness; die in darkness.

For those who die in Christ, the darkness has passed. "God is light; in him there is no darkness at all" (1 John 1:5 NIV). Live in light; die in light. No wonder we worship. No wonder we submit. No wonder we serve. I'm glad Charles Wesley did not back down from the bold assertion:

> *Amazing love! how can it be*
> *That Thou, my God, shouldst die for me?*

CHAPTER 5

A CRY OF
SUFFERING

"I am thirsty."

—JOHN 19:28 NIV

Imagine the Water of Life saying, "I am thirsty."

Back in 1968, as a student in Israel, I, along with some friends, trudged to the top of the fortress of Masada in 100° heat. Visualize the path that the ancient historian Josephus described as a "snake trail" winding its way up the side of a high mountain. We underestimated the amount of water we would need for the steep three-hour climb. Never before or since have I experienced such debilitating, burning, ravaging thirst.

Such thirst is not to be compared with the thirst of crucifixion, for crucifixion is a long slow process of dehydration.[1]

Beginning with Gethsemane, where Jesus sweat as it were great drops of blood; to His arrest; to His trials before Annas and Caiaphas; to His spending the night in a dungeon, with a new series of trials in the morning; to the flogging and being forced to carry His cross—such suffering would drain the fluids from His body. Now for six hours He had hung on the cross without moisture. I'm told that, in the Swedish language, the words for *thirst* and *fire* are related. Those who have been truly thirsty say that thirst can burn like fire in one's mouth.

How can the Creator of rivers and oceans have parched lips? How can Omnipotence thirst for a drink? How can the One who spoke the raging sea into submission long for a few drops of refreshment? Yes, the Man who is thirsty has all power in heaven and earth in His hands. He did miracles for others but would not perform one for Himself. He refused to turn stones into bread while hungering in the desert, and now He refused to create water while thirsting on the cross. He has taught us how to live; He will now teach us how to die.

The simple phrase "I am thirsty" has a world of meaning. He speaks for all who are thirsty, for all who have unmet desires. The drops of water for which He longed become for us showers of blessing. Let's reflect on what these words meant to Him and mean to us as His followers.

THE HUMANITY OF JESUS

His thirst proves that He was indeed a man. Although many in our society find it difficult to believe that Jesus was God, we as evangelicals struggle to accept His complete humanity. There is something scandalous about Jesus becoming fully man, even to the point of becoming tired and thirsty. Yet the

Scriptures assure us that He grew up as a child; He ate, slept, drank, and became weary. He became angry at injustice, and when overcome by sympathy, He wept.

The Definition of the Council of Chalcedon (AD 451) affirms that Christ was "truly God and truly man," with the two natures united in one person. He was not just a manifestation of God but rather "very God of very God," as the Nicene Creed puts it. Yet He was also man, with a human body, soul, and spirit. As God He could say, "Very truly I tell you . . . before Abraham was born, I am!" (John 8:58 NIV). As man He could say, "I am thirsty" (John 19:28 NIV). God the Father does not thirst; angels do not thirst. This was the thirst of a dying man.

We can't help but think that His thirst was not just the physical yearning for a drink of water. The trial of His soul affected His body as they sympathized with each other in His distress. "A joyful heart is good medicine, but a crushed spirit dries up the bones" (Proverbs 17:22). As Pink said, "His 'thirst' was *the effect* of the agony of His soul in the fierce heat of God's wrath."[2] Jesus' thirst expressed His yearning to be back in fellowship with the Father after three hours of horrid separation. David wrote, "As the deer pants for flowing streams, so my soul pants for you, O God. My soul thirsts for God, for the living God. When shall I come and appear before God?" (Psalm 42:1–2). Jesus' thirst for the Father's presence might have been greater than His thirst for water.

The agony of Jesus was predicted by David: "I am poured out like water, and all my bones are out of joint; my heart is like wax; it has melted within my breast; my strength is dried up like a potsherd, and my tongue sticks to my jaws; you lay me in the dust of death" (Psalm 22:14–15). He knows the meaning of the word *pain* not just as a physician knows about a disease, but as a man who suffered lacerated wounds and a parched mouth. The angels would have gladly brought Him water, but He will endure the dehydration.

He was thirsty that He might redeem us from an eternal thirst.

THE SUBMISSION OF JESUS

Why did Jesus not create a stream of water within His parched mouth? Why did He bother to say, "I am thirsty," when He was minutes away from death? The answer is that there was yet a prophecy that had to be fulfilled. Centuries earlier David had written, "They put gall in my food and gave me vinegar for my thirst" (Psalm 69:21 NIV). He had not yet been given vinegar, so Jesus, knowing that this detail could not be overlooked, called out, so that it would yet come to pass. We read, "Later, knowing that all was now finished, and so that the Scripture would be fulfilled, Jesus said, 'I am thirsty'" (John 19:28 NIV).

A soldier responded to the cry of Jesus, fulfilling the prophecy. "A jar of wine vinegar was there, so they soaked a sponge in it, put the sponge on a stalk of the hyssop plant, and lifted it to Jesus' lips" (v. 29 NIV). Jesus was crucified only perhaps two or three feet from the ground, so it would have been easy for a solider to put a sponge on a reed and hold it to His mouth. This vinegar was the cheap wine of the soldiers given only to wet His lips, but it fulfilled the prophecy.

He does not say, "I am thirsty," so that His raging thirst might be slaked. He cries out so that the Scriptures might be fulfilled. As F. W. Grant has written, "The terrible thirst of crucifixion is upon Him, but that is not enough to force those parched lips to speak; but it is written; 'In My thirst they gave Me vinegar to drink'—this opens them."³ Every detail, including the kind of drink given, had to come to pass as predicted. The soldier could not have given Him water; nor could the soldier have given Him new wine. If the prophecy called for vinegar, vinegar it must be.

Would we have given Jesus water if we had been there? Yes, we would have, we think. But He taught that we have that privilege even today:

> Come, you who are blessed by my Father, inherit the kingdom prepared for you from the foundation of the world. For I was hungry and you gave me food, I was thirsty and you gave me drink. . . . Truly, I say to you, as you did it to one of the least of these my brothers, you did it to me. (MATTHEW 25:34–35, 40)

If we give a cup of cold water to a member of Jesus' family, we are giving it to Him!

Jesus' burning thirst calls out to us about the depth of His submission to the Word of God. Jesus was resigned to whatever had been written; He accepted the plan He and the Father had agreed upon. We must ask whether we are as prepared to be as submissive to Him as He was to His Father. Are we willing to suffer unmet needs, even burning thirst? Are our comforts of more value to us than the Father's will? Is our spiritual thirst for God as great as our physical thirst for a glass of cold water in the blistering sun?

We've all been deprived of something we're convinced we can't do without. A new widow told me she does not know how she can go on without her husband. A man, cheated out of his inheritance, said that he does not know how to face his future robbed of the money that was rightfully his. Another is angry because he was denied the health care he believes he deserved. Nothing, however, can compare to being deprived of water when hanging crucified.

We've all noticed that it does not take much for us to have our fellowship with God interrupted. An unpleasant phone call, the need to skip a meal, a physical pain—all of these can make us question whether God has forsaken us. We grumble when we have no water, though in point of fact, we deserve a cup of the wrath of God.[4]

Jesus was submissive to the Father's will as recorded in the Father's Word. It mattered not whether it was pleasant or torturous. The glory of the Father overshadowed all suffering, pain, and injustice. Paul wrote, "Let each of us please his neighbor for his good, to build him up. For Christ did not please himself, but, as it is written: 'The reproaches of those who reproached you fell on me'" (Romans 15:2–3). Not our will, but God's matters.

THE SYMPATHY OF JESUS

I've spent countless hours trying to find an intellectual answer to the problem of evil; I've read the best minds who have tried to reconcile the suffering of this planet with God's love and care for the world. But even when I find an answer that makes sense to my mind, it still does not satisfy my heart, especially when I am the one who is suffering.

I know that God sees me; I know that He knows all things—that is an article of basic theology. But what I really want to know is whether God feels my pain. Standing at the foot of the cross, we need not wonder any longer. Jesus felt the pain of rejection, the pain of injustice, and, yes, the pain of thirst.

> For we do not have a high priest who is unable to sympathize with our weaknesses, but one who in every respect has been tempted as we are, yet without sin. Let us then with confidence draw near to the throne of grace, that we may receive mercy and find grace to help in time of need. (HEBREWS 4:15–16)

Here is proof that Jesus was not aloof from the common suffering of humanity.

Christ has entered into our world; He has participated in our suffering. He walked our planet, ate our food, drank our water, and felt our pain. Whatever we may be experiencing today, we can know with confidence that Jesus experienced all that and more. God has entered into our suffering world.

Are we in physical pain? Let us remember His burning thirst.

Has our dignity been assaulted? He was crucified naked.

Do we feel as if we are in darkness? So was He.

Do we feel forsaken? He was forsaken by the Father.

Jesus, the sinless Son of God, was, of course, perfect. But interestingly, He could only be perfect in His work through obedience to the Father's will. And, even more to the point, the will of the Father had to include suffering. "It is fitting that he, for whom and by whom all things exist, in bringing many sons to glory, should make the founder of their salvation perfect through suffering" (Hebrews 2:10). If Jesus needed to suffer to perfectly fulfill the will of God, why should we be exempt?

THIRST, SUFFERING, AND YOU

One of the first signs of life is thirst. We are all born thirsty, as every new mother knows. But just as we come into this world

93

with physical thirst, so we have a spiritual thirst built into the soul. Back in the sixteenth century, Henry Scougal wrote, "The soul of man . . . hath in it a raging and inextinguishable thirst."[5] Only when we give ourselves up to God can that thirst be satisfied. There is within us a thirst for fellowship, not just with other people, but with the God who created us. Understandably so, for we were created for His pleasure.

Some people are determined to quench that thirst through alcohol, sex, money, or power. Others exist on medication because they cannot bear the pain of their own emptiness. Some fill their lives with pleasure, trying to survive by continually igniting the sensations of the body. All of these watering holes give the illusion of nourishment, but they only inoculate a man and keep him from the true water. "They have forsaken me, the fountain of living waters, and hewed out cisterns for themselves, broken cisterns that can hold no water" (Jeremiah 2:13). The more affluent a society, the more broken cisterns lure the unsuspecting.

The issue is not whether we thirst—for we all do—but rather how *long* we will thirst. We've all speculated on what it must be like for those who are in hell. If they are able to speak, what are they saying? Jesus told a story to show how the fortunes of the rich and the poor might be reversed in eternity. He said that there was a beggar named Lazarus, who would eat the crumbs from under the rich man's table. When they died, the rich man went into the place of torment, and Lazarus went to the place of bliss. In fact, Lazarus, bless him, was in the company of Abraham.

Now, the rich man had no time for Lazarus when they were together in this world, but now that they were in eternity, he said to Abraham, "Father Abraham, have mercy on me, and send Lazarus to dip the end of his finger in water and cool my tongue, for I am in anguish in this flame" (Luke 16:24). What do people in hades (which will eventually be thrown into hell) *say?* Tormented in the fire they cry out, "I am thirsty!"

As Matthew Henry put it, "The torments of hell are represented by a violent thirst, in the complaint of the rich man who begged for a drop of water to cool his tongue. To that everlasting thirst we had all been condemned, if Christ had not suffered on the cross."[6] Hell is heightened desires with decreased satisfaction. Hell is the inflamed desires of the body, with no possibility of a drink. Hell is remembering the Living Water we could have enjoyed on earth that would have taken us to heaven. Hell is a lake of fire, a place of endless, unquenchable thirst.

Thankfully, Jesus suffered parched lips that we might be able to drink from the wells of salvation. He endured the thirst of hell, so that its fires might be quenched for us. Of those in heaven we read, "They shall hunger no more, neither thirst anymore; the sun shall not strike them, nor any scorching heat. For the Lamb in the midst of the throne will be their shepherd, and he will guide them to springs of living water, and God will wipe away every tear from their eyes" (Revelation 7:16–17).

Jesus drank from the cup of death that we might be able to drink from the cup of life. He drank the cup of wrath, that we might enjoy the cup of blessing. "Meet the thirsty Christ at the cross and your soul will never go thirsty again."[7] Take a drink of living water now, and you will enjoy it forever.

"There were three cups at Calvary," says Warren Wiersbe.[8] The first cup was offered to Him when He arrived at the cross. "They came to a place called Golgotha (which means 'the place of the skull'). There they offered Jesus wine to drink, mixed with gall; but after tasting it, he refused to drink it" (Matthew 27:33–34 NIV). The word *gall* has many meanings; in this context it refers to a poisonous herb, perhaps opium. This was wine, mingled with gall to form a sedative to ease the pain. This was the cup of *charity*, which He refused.

The second cup was the cup of *sympathy*. As we have already learned, when Jesus cried, "I am thirsty," a soldier dipped a sponge in vinegar, put it on a reed, and lifted it up to Him. Apparently, the moist sponge only touched His lips.

But there was a third cup that day on Skull Hill. It was the cup of *iniquity*, which Jesus drank to the dregs. "My Father, if it be possible, let this cup pass from me; nevertheless, not as I will, but as you will" (Matthew 26:39). Then, when Peter drew his sword to defend his Master, Jesus rebuked him, "Put your sword into its sheath; shall I not drink the cup that the Father has given me?" (John 18:11). This was the cup of God's wrath, filled to the brim.

This explains why He refused a sedative: He wanted to drink this cup completely and at full strength without spilling a single drop. This is the cup that He feared and yet chose to lift to His lips. This was the cup of iniquity, drunk dry for you and me.

> *Death and the curse were in our cup;*
> *O Christ, 'twas full for thee!*
> *But thou hast drain'd the last dark drop,*
> *'Tis empty now for me.*[9]

Earlier in His ministry, this Jesus who is now thirsty cried out, "If anyone thirsts, let him come to me and drink. Whoever believes in me, as the Scripture has said, 'Out of his heart will flow rivers of living water'" (John 7:37–38). He could promise the woman at the well living water because He knew He would personally bear her thirst. "Everyone who drinks of this water will be thirsty again, but whoever drinks of the water that I will give him will never be thirsty again. The water that I give him will become in him a spring of water welling up to eternal life" (John 4:13–14).

> *Jesus, in Thy thirst and pain*
> *While Thy wounds Thy lifeblood drain*
> *Thirsting more our love to gain:*
> *Hear us, holy Jesus.*
>
> *Thirst for us in mercy still;*
> *All Thy holy work fulfill;*
> *Satisfy Thy loving will:*
> *Hear us, holy Jesus.*
>
> *May we thirst Thy love to know;*
> *Lead us in our sin and woe*
> *Where the healing waters flow:*
> *Hear us, holy Jesus.*[10]

No wonder the last invitation in the Bible reads, "The Spirit and the Bride say, 'Come.' And let the one who hears say, 'Come.' And let the one *who is thirsty* come; let the one who desires take the water of life without price" (Revelation 22:17, emphasis added). Those who come to the One who was once thirsty need never thirst again.

CHAPTER 6

A CRY OF VICTORY

"It is finished."
—JOHN 19:30

You and I were born with an expiration date.

My friend Brandt Gustavson and his wife, Mary, were on a cruise when he took sick and went to the closest port for a checkup. The recommendation was that he fly back to the U.S. as soon as possible to confirm the diagnosis: cancer of the liver and pancreas. The doctors gave him two months to live, and they were right. Brandt, ever a realist, chose to use the weeks he had left to prepare his organization for an immediate transition and to plan his funeral. He did not spend his time searching for some exotic cure that promised healing. After all, if God did not want him to die, He could have prevented the cancer. Brandt was glad that he knew when he would die, so that he could both give and receive love from his family and friends. He died, without regrets, having finished his work.

You and I might not be fortunate enough to know exactly when we will transition from this life to the next. But ready or not, death will overtake us, gradually or suddenly. On that day the unavoidable question will be, Did we finish what God wanted us to do? Or, did we pretty well live as we pleased, with only a reverent nod in God's direction? How many of our opportunities were squandered, and how much did we leave unfinished? And what did we do that will stand the test of judgment day? Deny it as we wish, we shall be called to account.

Of course we all hope that we will be able to say that we have finished what God gave us to do, but only Jesus could say those words with absolute truthfulness. He died with the assurance that His assignment was completed perfectly and eternally. He died without a single regret. He did not need more time to preach one more sermon, heal one more paralytic, or create one more loaf of bread. He was only thirty-three but had finished His responsibilities down to the letter. Anything more would have been beyond His calling.

The sixth cry, "It is finished," followed quickly after His agonizing shout, "I am thirsty," and before that His cry of dereliction, "My God, my God, why have you forsaken me?" (Matthew 27:46; Mark 15:34; John 19:28, 30). Though He ended His earthly days with trauma, He would die with the satisfaction of knowing that the purpose for His coming had been successfully fulfilled.

In these words lies the assurance of our own salvation, the sure knowledge that our personal debt to the Father was paid by Another. Yes, of course Jesus had yet to be buried, rise again, and ascend into heaven. But that was a foregone conclusion. The difficult work of suffering, the difficult work of being separated from the presence of His Father, the difficult work of being treated like a sinner was over. There was nothing left in the flesh that He could do for God.

A dying man told me, "I have lived for myself all of my life; and now I have to face God." I assured him that Jesus died without regrets so that He could forgive our regrets. He completed His work, so that despite our uncompleted work, we might enter heaven. He successfully met God's standard to make up for our shortcomings. Yes, of course we should live for God all of our lives, but as the dying thief learned, even those with no good works can receive the gift of eternal life.

The sentence "It is finished" is but one word in Greek, *tetelestai*. The nineteenth-century preacher Charles Haddon Spurgeon said that this one word "would need all the other words that were ever spoken, or ever can be spoken, to explain it. . . . It is altogether immeasurable. It is high; I cannot attain to it. It is deep; I cannot fathom it."[1] Fathom it we cannot, but try we must.

The Greek word *tetelestai* comes from the verb *teleo*, which means "to bring to an end, to complete, to accomplish." It signifies a successful end to a particular course of action. You might have used the word after you had paid your bills or had run a race. A servant who completed his assignment would use the word to report back to his master. In short, it means that you have finished what you have set out to do.

Notice that the verb has no precise subject; in other words, we are not told specifically what was "finished" or "brought to completion." Yet it is clear that when He said, "It is finished," that little word *it* embodied the whole scope of our redemption. The rest of the New Testament fills in the blanks and reveals all we need to know about what was accomplished during those six hours on the cross. He spoke the words with a loud voice (this is seen in the parallel passages in Matthew 27:50 and Mark 15:37). He wanted the whole world to hear that special word which has echoed through twenty centuries. He did not say, "*I* am finished," for that would mean He died defeated. No, this was not the end for Him but the beginning of a new chapter in His eternal existence.

In shouting *"Tetelestai!"* Jesus gave the most triumphant cry in all of human history. He affirmed that He had successfully completed a great and mighty work. His life on earth closed, not as a failure but as the culmination of an eternal plan. The script had been written before Bethlehem, and now the curtain was about to close with everything in place (Luke 9:31; John 17:4).

Of course we have to ask more specifically, *What* was finished? Let's not limit the word to one part of His mission but see it as the fulfillment of God's grand plan of salvation. If Jesus had not finished it, we would be damned. But, thankfully, He did what He set out to do.

HIS SUFFERING WAS FINISHED

Let us remind ourselves that Jesus was born to suffer. He began His earthly career in an unpretentious stable in Bethlehem. His crib was a feeding trough and His pillow most likely straw. At the age of twelve He was found in the temple and said, "Did you not know that I must be about My Father's business?" (Luke 2:49 NKJV). And that business would include more than preaching and healing; it would include the business of paying the price of our redemption. His job description called for suffering according to the timetable agreed upon beforehand with His Father.

Though His close friends accepted Him, the wider society believed Him to be a nuisance at best and a demon-possessed troublemaker at worst. The religious authorities wanted to stone Him; others wanted to marginalize His growing ministry by ridicule and false accusations. Citizens of His hometown of Nazareth conspired to push Him over a cliff but could not do so because His time had "not yet come" (John 7:6). The rejection hurt.

That was now finished.

The secular powers of Rome cared nothing about what He believed, nor were its rulers fazed by His claims. They saw Him only as a threat to the stability of the Jewish society that was under their constant surveillance and control. They were glad to put Him through a series of mock trials and then do the dirty work of crucifying Him. What mattered was whether the Jewish authorities were appeased, not whether the verdict was fair. The injustice stung.

That was now finished.

As for His disciples, they professed loyalty but backed away when their commitment became costly. They knew it was dangerous and unwise to be the friends of someone who was hated and condemned and crucified. Judas kissed His cheek, but in that outward profession of love there was bitter betrayal. The other disciples (except John) ran to hide, hoping that they would not be the next conscripted for an appointment on Skull Hill. Their cowardice when He needed them the most, brought sadness.

That was now finished.

At the scene of the crime, we see the long spikes made of thorns pressing into His flesh; we remember the lacerations when He was tied to a pole and whipped. We remember how He staggered under the weight of His own cross. We recall the crucifixion with its pain and cruelty. We think of the separation from His Father and the burning thirst.

That was now finished.

Thankfully, His suffering had come to an end. And though His followers suffer for different reasons and in a different way, we can take heart that our suffering too shall someday be done with. Whatever we face today—whether it is our own impending death or an interminable emotional burden—someday we shall be able to say, "It is finished." To the woman whose husband has abandoned her, to the child whose father has mistreated her, to the person suffering from a terminal illness—to these we say that these wounds shall come to an end. The question is whether we have endured, with the sure knowledge that grief is a part of the divine plan. Jesus knew that, and so must we.

Much more than Jesus' suffering had come to an end. His focus was on the work His suffering accomplished. The mission for which He had set out on His journey from heaven to earth was finished.[2] All the details were carried out *"completely and irresistibly."*[3] Suffering was not an end in itself; the torment was a necessary part of the larger purpose of God. He had come to "save his people from their sins" (Matthew 1:21), and their salvation was now secure.

THE SACRIFICE WAS FINISHED

In Old Testament times, the people wondered when the sacrifices would be finished. Those who died in faith believed that the last payment for their sins was yet to be made. In fact, the Old Testament priests were not allowed to sit when they were on duty, symbolic of the fact that their work was never done. There was an endless stream of sacrifices; these cleansed the people in a ceremonial way but could not cleanse the conscience. Everyone knew that an animal could not substitute for a human being.

In the Old Testament, the priests offered sacrifices; but Jesus was both priest and sacrifice. His payment covered my indebtedness. Or, as Warren Wiersbe put it, "He took my bankruptcy and covered it with His solvency." He didn't just make a down payment and then expect me to keep up the installments. "But... he has appeared once for all at the end of the ages to put away sin by the sacrifice of himself" (Hebrews 9:26).

In ancient times, when the price of purchase was made and no debts were outstanding, written on the bill of sale was *Tetelestai,* "Paid in Full." On the cross, the justice of God was fully satisfied when our heavenly Substitute paid the great price of ransom. As Spurgeon put it, we can stand with confidence despite the thunder of the law and the lightening flash of justice, "for we are safe beneath the cross."[4] He paid the very last cent of the wages of our sin.

This means that my sins are on Jesus, not on me. Yes, there is sin *within* me but not *on* me. My sinful nature keeps luring me toward sin, and even in my best moments my works are tainted with selfish motives. But legally, I am accepted on the basis of the merit of Jesus. Figuratively speaking, I have a new set of clothes and a clear record in heaven. The righteousness of Jesus has been successfully credited to my account. God's justice has spent all of its ammunition; there is nothing left to be hurled at us.[5]

When on the Day of Atonement the high priest put his hand on the goat and confessed the sins of the nation upon the goat, the sins of the people were legally transferred to the animal. The beast was then taken into the wilderness where it was to be seen no more. This was symbolic of what God would do. Thanks to Jesus, "[my] sins and iniquities" God will "remember no more" (Hebrews 10:17 KJV).

> *Jesus paid it all,*
> *All to Him I owe;*
> *Sin had left a crimson stain,*
> *He washed it white as snow.*[6]

THE DEFEAT OF SATAN

"It is finished!"

That cry meant that the seed of the woman had triumphed over the loathsome serpent. Jesus affirmed, "Now is the judgment of this world; now will the ruler of this world be cast out" (John 12:31). The sentence has been passed, though it has not yet been executed.

How I wish a video camera had been able to record the drama that took place in the spiritual world that day on Calvary. A cosmic battle was fought. The devil was there, God was there, Christ was there, and we were there. Just read Paul's words, and I'll explain them in a moment.

> And you, who were dead in your trespasses and the uncircumcision of your flesh, God made alive together with him, having forgiven us all our trespasses, by canceling the record of debt that stood against us with its legal demands. This he set aside, nailing it to the cross. He

disarmed the rulers and authorities and put them to open
shame, by triumphing over them in him.
(COLOSSIANS 2:13–15)

Picture a courtroom scene. God is in there, and He
knows better than we the extent of our sins and guilt. The
devil, who is our accuser, shows up to make his case against
us. He reminds God that "the wages of sin is death" (Romans
6:23). He tells God, quite plausibly, that we would defile the
courts of heaven if we were admitted into those holy realms.
He tells the Almighty that He could be accused of associ-
ating with men who are unclean, which might call Jehovah's
holiness and truthfulness into question. The Evil One also
argues that we should have the same penalty as he; if he has
to suffer eternally for his sin, why should we who have also
sinned be exempt? If the greatness of the sin is determined
by the greatness of the One against whom it is committed,
then we are guilty of great transgressions.

Enter Christ.

Paul says that the decrees that were against us were
"nailed ... to the cross" (Colossians 2:14 NKJV). In those days,
when a criminal was hung on the cross, his crime had to be
publicly proclaimed. The list of transgressions was written
on a placard and nailed above the dying man. We've already
learned that Pilate had the notice, "Jesus of Nazareth, the
King of the Jews," fastened to the cross (John 19:19), indi-
cating the crime of which Jesus was accused.

This was the imagery Paul used to help us understand the
death of Christ on our behalf. He wanted us to imagine that
high above Pilate's words, there was a cosmic bulletin board
on which our sins were listed. Though we were not yet born,
the sins that we would commit two thousand years later were

recorded there. The list included everything Satan said about us, as well as other secret sins that were known but to an omniscient God. Only He knows the extent of our sins and the severity of the penalty they incurred.

When Jesus said, "Paid in full," the penalty credited to us was canceled. If God were still to expect a payment from us after Christ paid our debt, He would be unrighteous. Our debt was paid so completely that no further payment will ever become due.

God strips away Satan's arguments by pronouncing us FORGIVEN. The accusations of our enemy have been shown to be fraudulent. God "disarmed the powers and authorities" making them a "public spectacle" (Colossians 2:15 NIV). Just as Saul was stripped of his title as king yet pursued David for ten years, so Satan pursues us though he has been toppled by One greater than he. Only from our standpoint does there seem to be a gap between the victory of Christ over Satan and the final disposal of the defeated foe. Lightning and thunder take place at the same time, but we see the light before we hear the rumble. From God's standpoint both the victory and the judgment of the devil already took place on the cross. We have seen the lightning but are simply awaiting the crash of his fall.

Thanks to the defeat of Satan, we have switched kingdoms, "He has delivered us from the domain of darkness and transfered us to the kingdom of his beloved Son" (Colossians 1:13). If Satan cannot destroy us with guilt, he tries to destroy us with fear, particularly the fear of death, but that is futile. "Since the children have flesh and blood, he too shared in their humanity so that by his death he might break the power of him who holds the power of death—that is, the devil—and free those who all their lives were held in slavery by their fear of death" (Hebrews 2:14–15 NIV).

Yes, we fight Satan today, but the fight is fixed. The outcome is not in doubt.

SINNERS ASSURED OF HEAVEN

Since believers do not owe God any righteousness, their permanent acceptance by God has been secured. In the Colossian passage already referred to, we read, "He forgave us all our sins" (Colossians 2:13 NIV). How many of our sins were future when Christ died? Obviously, all of them. And what about the sins you will commit tomorrow and the day after? The answer, of course, is that for those who believe on Christ, even future sins are forgiven. If it were not so, we could not be sure of our eternal salvation.

Of course we must still confess our sins, not to maintain our status as sons and daughters of the Almighty but to maintain our fellowship with the Father. And if we do not walk in obedience, we will be disciplined. But for those who believe, their sins have legally been blotted out. We can rejoice in the security of our salvation, because we have been acquitted, completely and forever. "But when Christ had offered for all time a sngle sacrifice for sins, he sat down at the right hand of God. . . . For by a single offering he has perfected for all time those who are being sanctified" (Hebrews 10:12, 14). Though we might well weep when we repent of our sins, not even tears can be added to the finished work of Jesus.

Put your sin in the ledger and write "Paid in Full" next to it.

- An abortion: Paid in Full.
- Fornication: Paid in Full.

- Cheating: Paid in Full.
- Greed: Paid in Full.
- Abandoning responsibilities: Paid in Full.
- Criminal behavior: Paid in Full.
- Selfishness: Paid in Full.

If I've overlooked your sin, you can add it to the list. Truth be told, we have no idea of the number of our sins, for we can neither remember them nor recognize all of them as sinful. And, of course, the greatest sin is our selfish failure to follow the command, "Love the Lord your God with all your heart and with all your soul and with all your mind" (Matthew 22:37). No wonder we read, "For all have sinned and fall short of the glory of God" (Romans 3:23). Thankfully, we have a real Savior who saves us from real sins.

No wonder Jesus taught that the number of the redeemed will be comparatively small! We are so prone to add our own goodness to what Jesus did that it is difficult to grasp the wonder of grace. The way to heaven is narrow, and the way to destruction is broad. Those who embrace Christ's work for themselves have the confidence that their eternal destiny is secure. For if we believe that Jesus did all that ever will be necessary for us to stand before God, and we accept Him as dying for us, we will be saved and know it. Someone has written,

> *Upon a Life I did not live*
> *Upon a Death I did not die*
> *Another's death—Another's life*
> *I cast my soul eternally.*

Count Nikolaus Ludwig von Zinzendorf speaks the words for us today:

Bold shall I stand in Thy great day,
For who aught to my charge shall lay?
Fully absolved through these I am
From sin and fear, from guilt and shame.[7]

THE PAYMENT WAS ACCEPTED

If the cry *Tetelestai!* was the Bondservant reporting to His Master about the status of His assignment, then we can be sure that the Father agreed with the Son that the atonement had been made. No sooner did the Son give His final cry than we read, "The curtain of the temple was torn in two, from top to bottom. And the earth shook, and the rocks were split" (Matthew 27:51). The way to God was now open. Instead of entry being restricted to the high priest entering the Holy of Holies on only one day in the year, entrance into God's presence was now available to all who came through Christ. With the barrier of our sin taken away, we can now "draw near . . . by the blood of Christ" (Hebrews 10:22 with Ephesians 2:13).

Later, Jesus was laid into a tomb belonging to Joseph of Arimathea. But when His disciples visited His resting place, they discovered the stone rolled away and the body of Jesus gone! Later, He revealed Himself to them, and they realized that He was raised from the dead. This was proof, if proof were needed, that the Father accepted the sacrifice of the Son. This was the Son in whom the Father was "well pleased."

Forty days later, Jesus was taken up into heaven from the Mount of Olives. There He reigns, not just by virtue of who He is but also by virtue of what He had accomplished.

MY APPEAL TO YOU

If you, my friend, have never received Christ as your personal sin bearer, I urge you to do so right now. The issue before you is not the greatness of your sin but the worth of the sacrifice Jesus provided. Timothy McVeigh was not beyond redemption. We have no evidence that he accepted Christ, but if he had, he too could have been forgiven, just as surely as the most committed saint. Of course it is better that you live a good life rather than that of a criminal. But at the end of the day, it is the payment that Christ made that saves, and not our lifestyle. There is nothing left for us to do except receive the free gift.

If we add to what Jesus did by spiritual rituals, penance, or pilgrimages, we actually subtract from it. Philip Ryken points out that just like we cannot add a *g* to the word *love* without changing its meaning (in this case the word becomes *glove*), just so, we cannot add to what Jesus did by depending on own good intentions or good works.[8] To add to Jesus' gift is to destroy it altogether. God does not want our worthiness but our *willingness* to accept Christ's payment on our behalf.

One man told me with breathtaking confidence, "I want to stand before God on the basis of my own record." I assured him that that would be like standing within a hundred yards of the sun. He would be blinded by the holiness of God and cast aside into an eternal hell of personal suffering and humiliation. And so his punishment would last forever, he would never be able to say, "It is finished!" Rather, he would cry, "It is *not* finished!" Jesus did in six hours what no human being can do in all of eternity. God's justice on behalf of those who reject His Son shall never be satisfied, for the simple reason that only He can meet His own demands.

The good news is that we do not have to pin our rags to

the fine linen of Jesus' righteousness. Spurgeon asked, "Why will you add your counterfeit farthing to the costly ransom which Christ has paid into the treasure-house of God?"[9] No wonder we sing:

> *Lifted up was He to die,*
> *"It is finished," was His cry;*
> *Now in heaven exalted high;*
> *Hallelujah! what a Saviour.*[10]

Thankfully, those who trust Christ have the assurance that "it is finished."

CHAPTER 7

A CRY OF SUBMISSION

*"Father, into your hands
I commit my spirit."*

—LUKE 23:46

L ast words.
A missionary told me that in African culture the national Christians pray that they will die a "good death." Contrary to what we might think, a "good death" is not dying without pain, or dying with dignity, or even necessarily dying in old age. A "good death" is having the opportunity of gathering one's family around one last time and having the strength to give them a final "charge" to live a godly life and to prepare for a reunion in heaven. The faith is passed on as the dying affirm their faith to the living.

What would *our* last words be?

When we learn how Jesus died, we will never think of death in the same way again. He who went before us showed us the way and invites us to join Him in the world beyond. The darkness was forever over; the suffering was finished, and now He was finally able to commit His spirit into the hands of His Father whose sweet presence has returned. He left us the legacy of a "good death."

The spirit is the highest part of us. Animals have souls, but only mankind has a spirit that makes fellowship with God possible. At death our spirit will depart somewhere, either to the light of eternal day or the darkness of eternal night. Jesus commended His spirit to the Father, placing Himself with assurance into the Father's care. And the good news is that you and I can die with the same confidence.

Where did the spirit of Jesus go at death? His spirit—with its desires, aspirations, and affections—went to the Father in paradise, there to prepare to meet the thief who would be arriving later that day. This is His human spirit or, better, the spirit of the God-man returning to the Father's fellowship and presence. This spirit would be united to the body of Jesus three days later at the time of the resurrection. Thus when Paul prays in 1 Thessalonians 5:23 that our "whole spirit and soul and body be kept blameless," it is the unity of who we are that is preserved. Like Jesus, our spirits shall be safely guided to the Father, and later our bodies will be raised.

Interestingly, none of the New Testament writers are content to simply say that Jesus died; they all say that His spirit went into the hands of God. They want us to understand that His death was not the end but the beginning of a new relationship. If we learn from our Master, we will be ready when our final hour comes. He died in faith and was rewarded.

In ancient times a forerunner would help a vessel enter the harbor safely. He would jump from the ship, wade to the harbor, and fasten the strong rope of the ship to a rock along the shore. Then by means of a winch, the vessel was brought in. This is the imagery used by the author of Hebrews, who views Jesus as the One who has gone to heaven to prepare the way for us. "We have this as a sure and steadfast anchor for the soul, a hope that enters into the inner place behind the curtain, where Jesus has gone as a forerunner on our behalf" (Hebrews 6:19–20). Let storms tear our sails to shreds; let the floors creak; let the gusts of wind attempt to blow us off course; the redeemed shall arrive safely at port. Each day we are pulled a notch closer to the harbor by the One who has proved that He is stronger than death.

HE DIED IN HIS FATHER'S PRESENCE

Here on earth, Jesus lived in the presence of the Father, but now He would return to the Father's immediate fellowship and glory. This, His last loud cry, expressed confidence that He would be welcomed into the heavenly realms. We've learned that for the first three hours on the cross He suffered under the hands of men; during the last three hours He suffered under the hands of God. And now it is into those same hands He now entrusts His spirit.

Note well: Jesus was just as committed to suffer in His Father's hands as He was to rejoice in His Father's hands. The hands that brought the suffering would now bring joy and relief. The first recorded words of Jesus were, "Did you not know that I must be about My Father's business?" (Luke 2:49 NKJV). Now that His Father's business is finished, His last words would be, "Father, into thy hands I commend my spirit" (Luke 23:46 KJV). From beginning to end, this Son cared only about one thing: doing the Father's will and finishing it. He had made known the Father's name to His disciples; He had become sin for those who would believe on Him. Nothing was left undone.

Jesus died while meditating on the Scriptures. When King David was defamed and persecuted, he exhorted all who would listen to be strong, knowing that the Lord would protect them in a time of crisis. The Lord was his refuge and would not put him to shame. Then he added, "Into thine hand I commit my spirit: thou hast redeemed me, O Lord God of truth" (Psalm 31:5 KJV). How fitting that these were the final words spoken by Jesus while in His earthly body. He died with the assurance that God would take care of what was entrusted to Him.

HE DIED WITHIN HIS FATHER'S PROVIDENCE

Even with His dying breath, Jesus was still King. The One who said that no man could take His life from Him died at the appointed time and in the appointed way. In the Old Testament the literal statement for the moment when the Passover Lamb was to be killed was "between the evenings," which according to Jewish tradition was somewhere between three in the afternoon and six in the evening ("twilight," Exodus 12:6 NIV). Jesus was crucified on the exact day that the Passover lambs were being killed (John 18:28). At 3:00 p.m. He cried His last, fulfilling His role as "the Lamb of God, who takes away the sin of the world" (John 1:29).

We should not be surprised that His death was an act of personal volition, a choice He made. Matthew does not record the last words of Jesus but says simply, "And Jesus cried out again with a loud voice and yielded up his spirit" (Matthew 27:50). His spirit was under His control until He voluntarily "gave it up" to the Father. His life was not wrested from Him by the throes of death. The phrase can also be translated that He "dismissed" His spirit. This expression is most appropriate in Matthew, where Jesus is presented as the King.

As King, Jesus was always in control. He was in control when He was asleep on the boat; He was in control when soldiers came to arrest him. Pilate thought himself to be in control, but Jesus assured him that he was mistaken. "Pilate said to him, . . . 'Do you not know that I have authority to release you and authority to crucify you?' Jesus answered him, 'You would have no authority over me at all unless it had been given you from above'" (John 19:10–11). Pilate's power was a gift from God that could be taken away at will. Only what the Father and the Son agreed upon would come to pass.

John also records that Jesus "gave up his spirit" (v. 30). He delivered up His spirit to the Father because His blood had been shed, prophecies had been fulfilled, and the agreed upon schedule was completed. His death was not an accident but an appointment. He remained as Master of Himself, unconquered by death.

Jesus died according to the purposes of Divine Providence, not the whims of cowardly men. Just so, you and I will die, not according to the will of cancer, not according to the will of an erratic drunk cruising along the highway, not according to the will of a painful disease. We will die under the good hand of God's providential care. We will pass through the curtain according to God's clock, not the timetable of random fate.

HE DIED IN THE FATHER'S HANDS

"Father, into *your hands* . . ."

What a world of meaning is locked in that expression!

The power of hands. Repeatedly, Jesus said He was being delivered up into the hands of men. To His weary disciples in Gethsemane, He said, "See, the hour is at hand, and the Son of Man is betrayed into the hands of sinners. Rise, let us be going; see, my betrayer is at hand" (Matthew 26:45–46). Peter said that Jesus was crucified by "wicked men" (Acts 2:23 NIV). Wicked hands formed a crown of thorns and put it on His brow. Wicked hands lacerated His back. Wicked hands slapped Him. Wicked hands shoved Him. Wicked hands put nails through His hands and feet.

But there comes a time when the hands of men can do nothing more and God's hands have the final say.[1] When David was pursued by enemies, he realized that even when we are in the hands of wicked men, we are really in the hands of God. "My times are in your hands; rescue me from the hand of my enemies and from my persecutors!" (Psalm 31:15). Just so, ultimately, we are not in the hands of accidents or the apparent randomness of ill health. We are in the hands of God.

Jesus voluntarily gave Himself into the hands of sinners; now He voluntarily gives Himself into the hands of God. Surrounded by those who hated Him, knowing that the injustices against Him were as yet unaddressed, knowing that His disciples had for the most part deserted Him—in these circumstances He could count on His Father to receive His spirit. In the Father's hands He was elevated to a position of authority and today is waiting for His enemies to become a footstool for His feet.

Jesus teaches us that death is the door by which we are admitted into the presence of the King. He also reminds us that it is possible to die young and yet to have fulfilled the will of God. The more closely we walk with God, the more easily we will believe that He can be trusted with our spirit— that part of us that is the seat of our thinking, willing, caring, and feeling. Yes, of course, we want to be buried, as proof of our belief in the resurrection. Regardless of what becomes of our body, our spirit can return safely home. Come what may, we too shall be welcomed into the inner sanctum of the Father's presence.

> *Plagues and deaths around me fly,*
> *Till He please I cannot die;*
> *Not a single shaft can hit*
> *Till the God of love sees fit.*[2]

Surely, Paul must have been thinking about this when he wrote, "For I know whom I have believed, and am persuaded that he is able to keep that which I have committed unto him against that day" (2 Timothy 1:12 KJV).

If we are in the hands of the Father, we are also in the hands of the Son. Earlier in His ministry Jesus said to His disciples,

> "My sheep hear my voice, and I know them, and they follow me. I give them eternal life, and they shall never perish, and no one will snatch them out of my hand. My Father, who has given them to me, is greater than all, and no one is able to snatch them out of the Father's hand. I and the Father are one." (JOHN 10:27–30)

The hands of the Father and the Son are in harmony. How comforting to know that we are held by both, for the hand of the Father and the hand of the Son are locked together.

This seventh cry, this victorious shout, comes ringing to us through the centuries. Jesus had been asked to "save himself," but He persevered and then went home to the Father. Sin has been conquered; death has been proven powerless. There is a tribe in Africa in which, when a believer dies, they do not say, "He departed," but rather, "He arrived." And so it is; believers arrive in the home prepared by Jesus.

LIFE-CHANGING LESSONS

Death is not the *end* of the road, but simply a *bend* in the road. On a plane a person told me, "I don't believe in life after death . . . I don't believe that the soul survives the body." I replied, "You create a real problem for me. I have to make a choice between your view of ultimate reality and the opinion of Jesus; don't be offended, but I'm going with Him." We have to press the point that anyone who does not believe that the soul survives the body is at odds with Jesus, who had reason to speak with authority, "I am the first and the last, and the living one. I died, and behold I am alive forevermore, and I have the keys of Death and Hades" (Revelation 1:17–18).

Second, if your spirit does not go into the hands of God for safekeeping, it will go into the hands of God for judgment. The same hands that speak of hope and comfort also speak of terror and punishment. We are warned, "It is a fearful thing to fall into the hands of the living God" (Hebrews 10:31). The hands that are today outstretched, inviting us to receive mercy, are the hands that will throw the unrepentant into the pit of loneliness, despair, and the boredom of eternal suffering.

Before Timothy McVeigh was executed, he said he would have plenty of company in hell. One woman who was interviewed agreed that he would have company there with the likes of Hitler and Stalin. She was quite correct, but it would be a mistake to think that only such criminals will be in eternal punishment. Hell will be filled with many people who paid their taxes, refused to commit immorality, and were never charged with a crime. In short, all those who do not come under the protection of Christ's righteousness will eventually be separated from Him in conscious torment. That explains why Jesus said that the way to life was narrow and "few there be that find it" (Matthew 7:14 KJV).

Don't be wrong about whether or not you are in God's protective hands. When John Hus was condemned by the Council of Constance in 1415, the bishop ended the ceremony with, "Now we commit your soul to the devil." But Hus replied, "I commit my spirit into thy hands, Lord Jesus Christ; unto thee I commend my spirit, which thou hast redeemed."[3] Hus, who was a follower of Christ and understood the good news of the gospel, knew that no man can commit us into the hands of the devil if we have committed ourselves into the hands of God. He was burned at the stake, triumphant in the knowledge that he belonged to Christ and Christ belonged to him.

Perhaps you are thinking, *I will live as I please, and then at the last minute I will say, "Father, into Your hands I commit my spirit."* No, with few exceptions, you will die as you have lived. If God is not your Father now, it well might be impossible to accept Him as your Father as death draws near. We are prepared for heaven when we embrace Christ as our sin bearer, accepting what He did on the cross for us. Only those who so believe in Jesus can entrust their spirits to the Father with integrity.

Finally, God does not promise a calm passage through

the pathway of death, but He does promise a safe landing. Review once more the circumstance in which Jesus spoke these words. Those around Him jeered, denying Him the serene contemplation we would all want in our final moments. His body was bloody and crumpled; He was marred beyond recognition with ghastly scars and the contortions of dehydration. Pain numbed His body, and, for a time, the Father's presence had left Him.

Yet, His spirit is preserved. I've seen strong men dwindle down to one hundred pounds when cancer ravaged the body. I've seen people so disfigured in auto accidents that the family was not allowed to view the body. I've read a story about a farmer caught in machinery and hacked to bits.

Yes, some do die peacefully in a hospital room or even at home surrounded by friends. But multitudes die violent deaths; others are lost in the ocean or die unheralded in remote jungles.

The promise is that no matter how turbulent the death, we will arrive safely at our destination. We have the sure knowledge that the spirit survives the body, and thanks to the resurrection, our decaying bodies shall be raised to newness of life. We will be the same people in heaven as we are on earth. Yes, of course, sin will be removed, but we will carry our memories into the next life; we will also be aware of the attachments, friends, and relatives we had here.

Never shall the cross be so precious to us as when death is near. For if we have embraced the Christ who hung there for us, we shall never really die. For He died, not merely that our sins would be taken away but to prove that death does not have the last word for those whose faith is in the One who conquered it. "Since the children have flesh and blood, he too shared in their humanity so that by his death he might break the power of him who holds the power death—that is, the devil—and free those who all their lives were held in slavery by their fear of death" (Hebrews 2:14–15 NIV).

Many of the saints have died with these last words of Jesus on their lips. When the stones began to fly, Stephen, the first Christian martyr, prayed, "Lord Jesus, receive my spirit" (Acts 7:59). This is the only time in the New Testament that we read that Jesus was "standing at the right hand of God" ready to receive His servant (v. 55). He is there waiting for us as well. When D. L. Moody died, he said, "Earth recedes; Heaven opens for me. . . . If this is death, it is sweet."[4]

"Father, into your hands I commit my spirit."

TAKING THE CROSS INTO THE WORLD

It may take a crucified church to bring a crucified Christ before the eyes of the world," wrote W. E. Orchard.[1] The well-known atheist Nietzsche, when speaking of Christians, said, "I might believe in their redeemer if they were to look more redeemed!" The simple reality is that the message of the gospel must be authenticated to the world through the lives of Christ's followers. It does no good to protest that all that we need to do is preach the message; unless we live it, the world will find no reason to believe.

What did Jesus mean when He said that we should carry our cross? Surely this does not refer to enduring common illnesses, or the usual trouble associated with life itself. The unsaved have all of these experiences too. I believe that the cross we are given refers to the trouble we would not have if we were not Christians. Or, to put it positively, to carry our cross means to bear up under difficulties we have on our shoulders because we are followers of Jesus. The world hated Him; it will also hate us. The world put Him to death; the world will also try to destroy anyone who intends to share the message of the cross in word and deed.

If I were to expand on what it means to carry our cross, that would be another book. My plea to you is simply this: Since Jesus did so much for you, does it not make sense that we choose to live our lives for His glory alone, no matter the cost? Since the cross was an instrument of suffering for Him, should it not also be so for us?

Jesus did not save the world through His miracles. Miracles are never permanent. Even Lazarus had to die a second time. Jesus changed the world through suffering. We think that if we had the power to do miracles we would be able to change the world. Christ used such power to change the lives of a few people, but when He wanted to do the greater work—the grand work of redemption—only suffering brought about the desired result. Thus we must follow Christ in His weakness that we might be strong. As Dietrich Bonhoeffer said, "Christianity is a religion of suffering; a man throws himself into the arms of God and awakes in Gethsemane. We must leave our cherished dreams at the feet of our crucified Savior."

Since Christ died for what he believed, should we not follow His footsteps? Bonhoeffer also wrote:

The cross is laid on every Christian. The first Christ-suffering which every man must experience is the call to abandon the attachments of this world. It is that dying of the old man which is the result of his encounter with Christ. As we embark upon discipleship we surrender ourselves to Christ in union with his death—we give over our lives to death. Thus it begins; the cross is not the terrible end to an otherwise God-fearing and happy life, but it meets us at the beginning of our communion with Christ. When Christ calls a man, he bids him come and die. . . . Only the man who is dead to his own will can follow Christ.[2]

The cross represents the great "reversal of values": it stands a permanent witness to the fact that what men hate, God loves; and what He loves, men hate. Our willingness to identify with Christ in our homes, at work, and in our neighborhoods is an indispensable mark of a redeemed life. When the world sees us, they should be surprised, taken aback, and forced to take note. We should live as though from another country, with a different set of values, different aspirations, and a different interpretation of life itself. Just as Jesus was both loved and hated, both obeyed and reviled, so we should expect the same. "Remember the word that I said to you, 'A servant is not greater than his master.' If they persecuted Me, they will also persecute you. If they kept My word, they will keep yours also" (John 15:20 NKJV).

Christ's descent from heaven to earth represents the greatest act of condescension. He embarked on a slope that would take Him from the heights to the depths. And if we represent Him well, we will follow in His footsteps.

If we are as selfish as the world—if we angrily insist on our rights and make a spectacle of the insults we receive, either real or imagined—we will be indistinguishable from our culture. The world is not impressed when we malign them with overtones of political self-interest. Remember, that at the end of the day, what the world really needs is to see Jesus.

Chosen suffering, that is, our willingness to be identified with the poor, the outcasts, and the grieved, is most precious to God. During the holocaust, Dietrich Bonhoeffer asked his fellow Germans, "Who is Jesus Christ for us?" For them it was the Jews. For us, Jesus Christ might be:

The unborn child and the terrified teenager who knows not where to turn

The single mother who needs someone to give her son a male bonding experience

The biracial child who is ridiculed

The homosexual who is so overcome with guilt that he is contemplating suicide

The inmates in a local prison

The people in our inner cities

These are Jesus Christ to us today. But so is our alderman, the president, the mayor, the cab driver. Everyone we are quick to criticize is Christ for us today. We need to take our place and accept the role of a servant; we must be willing to die that others might live.

Bishop Samuel, who died in a hail of gunfire with Anwar Sadat of Egypt back in the early 1980s, told Dr. Ray Bakke how Christianity captured North Africa in the early centuries. He spoke about the love of the Christians that defied explanation. For example, in those days there were no abortion procedures, so unwanted children were just left to die on the streets. And since there were no baby bottles, nursing mothers gathered in the town square. Then there would be "baby runs"—young men seeking abandoned infants. These were brought to the nursing mothers, who adopted them as their own.

The despised Christians were often recruited as garbage collectors. When they found dead bodies (often the result of the plague), they would wash the bodies and give them a decent burial, arguing that even the wicked deserve a decent burial in light of the resurrection. The pagans were impressed with these unexplained acts of love.

Yes, if we expect people to believe in our Redeemer, we are going to have to look more redeemed. And to look more redeemed, we will have to follow our Redeemer to the cross. Let us lay aside our weapons and embrace the cross, not just as our means of salvation but as a way of living. Only then can we expect to bring hope to our hurting world.

NOTES

Preface

1. Fanny Jane Crosby (1820–1915), "Near the Cross."

A Journey into the Heart of Jesus

1. Sir Robert Anderson, *The Gospel and Its Mission* (Grand Rapids: Kregel, 1978), 26.
2. Herbert Butterfield, quoted in *The NIV Worship Bible* (Grand Rapids: Zondervan, 2000), 1455; notation for John 19.
3. P. T. Forsythe, *The Work of the Cross* (Hodder & Stoughton, 1910), quoted in John Stott, *The Cross of Christ* (Downers Grove, Ill.: InterVarsity, 1986), 44.
4. John Piper, *The Pleasures of God* (Portland, Ore.: Multnomah, 1991), 164.
5. Fanny Jane Crosby (1820–1915), "My Saviour First of All," chorus.
6. Robert Wassenar, "A Physician Looks at the Suffering of Christ," *Moody Monthly*, March 1979, 42.

7. Brooke Foss Wescott, quoted in *The NIV Worship Bible*, 1446 notation for John 12.
8. Richard Foster, *Prayer: Finding the Heart's True Home* (San Francisco: Harper, 1992), 1, quoted in Brennan Manning, *Abba's Child* (Colorado Springs: NavPress, 1994), 16.
9. Isaac Watts (1674–1748), "When I Survey the Wondrous Cross."
10. Edward Shillito, "Jesus of the Scars," *Aeropagus Proclamation* 10, no. 7 (April 2000).

Chapter 1: A Cry for Pardon

1. From a sermon by Warren Wiersbe, delivered at Moody Church, February, 1978.
2. William Bright, *The Seven Sayings from the Cross* (London: Parker, 1887), 19–20.
3. Charles Wesley (1707–88), "Arise, My Soul, Arise!"
4. Arthur W. Pink, *The Seven Sayings of the Saviour on the Cross* (Swengel, Pa.: Bible Truth Depot, 1954), 16.
5. Dietrich Bonhoeffer, "Vengeance and Deliverance," July 11, 1937, in *A Testament to Freedom: The Essential Writings of Dietrich Bonhoeffer*, rev. ed., ed. Geffrey B. Kelly and F. Burton Nelson (San Francisco: Harper, 1990, 1995), 282.
6. Jim Nance, "Stauron: His Prayer from the Cross," *Credena* 7, no. 4, 20.
7. Clarence Cranford, *The Seven Last Words* (Grand Rapids: Baker, 1960), 16.

Chapter 2: A Cry of Assurance

1. Arthur W. Pink, *The Seven Sayings of the Saviour on the Cross* (Swengel, Pa.: Bible Truth Depot, 1954), 31–32.
2. Ibid., 34.
3. Ibid., 29.
4. For the Scripture text of these taunts, see Matthew 27:42, 43, 44; Mark 15:29–30, 31–32; Luke 23:35, 36.
5. Charles Haddon Spurgeon, *Christ's Words from the Cross*, (Grand Rapids: Zondervan, 1993), 33.
6. William Cowper (1731–1800), "God Moves in a Mysterious Way."
7. Clarence Cranford, *The Seven Last Words* (Grand Rapids: Baker, 1960), 24.
8. William Cowper (1731–1800), "There Is a Fountain Filled with Blood."

Chapter 3: A Cry of Compassion

1. Samuel Johnson, quoted in James Boswell, *Life of Samuel Johnson* (1791), September 19, 1777.
2. William Barclay, *The Gospel of John*, vol. 2, *The Daily Study Bible* (Edinburgh: St. Andrew, 1965), 299.

3. Charles Swindoll, *The Darkness and the Dawn: Empowered by the Tragedy and Triumph of the Cross* (Nashville: Word, 2001), 153–54.
4. Arthur W. Pink, *The Seven Sayings of the Saviour on the Cross* (Swengel, Pa.: Bible Truth Depot, 1954), 49.
5. Ibid., 56.
6. Fanny Jane Crosby (1820–1915), "Near the Cross."
7. Dietrich Bonhoeffer, *The Cost of Discipleship*, 2d ed., revised and unabridged (New York: Macmillan, 1958), 79.

Chapter 4: A Cry of Anguish

1. John Stott, *The Cross of Christ* (Downers Grove, Ill.: InterVarsity, 1986), 151.
2. Arthur W. Pink, *The Seven Sayings of the Saviour on the Cross* (Swengel, Pa.: Bible Truth Depot, 1954), 70.
3. Isaac Watts (1674–1748), "Alas! and Did My Saviour Bleed?"
4. Pink, *The Seven Sayings of the Saviour on the Cross*, 64–84; but especially 65, 67, 69, 71, 75, regarding this paragraph.
5. Dennis Ngien, "The God Who Suffers," *Christianity Today* (February 3, 1997), 40.
6. Dietrich Bonhoeffer, Letter to Eberhard Bethge from Tergel Prison, 16 July 1944, in *Letters and Papers from Prison*, revised and enlarged ed.; Eberhard Bethge ed. (New York: Macmillan, 1953, 1967, 1971), 361.
7. Pink, *The Seven Sayings of the Saviour on the Cross*, 75.
8. Stott, *The Cross of Christ*, 79.
9. John Piper, "The Glory of Christ's Incomparable Sufferings," *The Standard*, (October 1999): 24.
10. Charles Wesley (1707–1788), "And Can It Be that I Should Gain?"
11. P. T. Forsyth, *The Work of Christ* (Hodder & Stoughton, 1910), quoted in Stott, *The Cross of Christ*, 153.
12. Pink, *The Seven Sayings of the Saviour on the Cross*, 80.
13. Charles Haddon Spurgeon, *Christ's Words from the Cross* (Grand Rapids: Zondervan, 1963), 67.

Chapter 5: A Cry of Suffering

1. Philip Graham Ryken, "Human After All," in *The Heart of the Cross*, James Montgomery Boice and Philip Graham Ryken (Wheaton, Ill.: Crossway, 1999), 37.
2. Arthur W. Pink, *The Seven Sayings of the Saviour on the Cross* (Swengel, Pa.: Bible Truth Depot, 1954), 91.
3. F. W. Grant, quoted in Pink, *The Seven Sayings of the Saviour on the Cross*, 94.
4. Pink, *The Seven Sayings of the Saviour on the Cross*, 95.
5. Henry Scougal, *The Life of God in the Soul of Man* (Harrisonburg, Va.: Sprinkle, 1986), 108, quoted in John Piper, *The Pleasures of God* (Portland: Multnomah, 1991), 13.

6. Matthew Henry, quoted in Ryken, "Human After All," in *The Heart of the Cross*, 42.
7. Ryken, "Human After All," in *The Heart of the Cross*, 42–43.
8. From a sermon by Warren Wiersbe, delivered at Moody Church, March 1978.
9. Anne (Annie) Ross Cundell Cousin (1824–1906), "O Christ, What Burdens Bowed Thy Head."
10. Thomas Benson Pollock (1836–96), "Jesus, in Thy Dying Woes," (1870), stanzas 12–14; text from http://www.cyberhymnal.org.

Chapter 6: A Cry of Victory

1. Charles Haddon Spurgeon, quoted by Philip Graham Ryken, "Mission Accomplished," in *The Heart of the Cross*, James Montgomery Boice and Philip Graham Ryken (Wheaton, Ill.: Crossway, 1999), 53.
2. Arthur W. Pink, *The Seven Sayings of the Saviour on the Cross* (Swengel, Pa.: Bible Truth Depot, 1954), 110.
3. Ibid., 112.
4. Charles Haddon Spurgeon, *Christ's Words from the Cross* (Grand Rapids: Zondervan, 1993), 102.
5. Ibid., 94.
6. Elvina Mabel Hall (1820–1889), "Jesus Paid It All," chorus.
7. Count Nikolaus Ludwig von Zinzendorf (1700–1760), trans. John Wesley (1703–1791), "Jesus, Thy Blood and Righteousness."
8. Ryken, "Mission Accomplished," in *The Heart of the Cross*, 57–58.
9. Spurgeon, *Christ's Words from the Cross*, 100.
10. Philip P. Bliss (1838–1876), "Hallelujah, What a Saviour!"

Chapter 7: A Cry of Submission

1. From a sermon by Warren Wiersbe, delivered at Moody Church, March, 1978.
2. Quoted in Charles Haddon Spurgeon, *Christ's Words from the Cross* (Grand Rapids: Zondervan, 1993), 119.
3. James Montgomery Boice, "Homeward Bound," in *The Heart of the Cross*, James Montgomery Boice and Philip Graham Ryken (Wheaton, Ill.: Crossway, 1999), 65.
4. Dwight L. Moody, quoted in A. P. Fitt, *The Life of D. L. Moody* (Chicago: Moody, n.d.), 122.

Epilogue: Taking the Cross into the World

1. W. E. Orchard, *In the Temple*, quoted in *Christianity Today* (April 9, 1990), 38.
2. Dietrich Bonhoeffer, *The Cost of Discipleship*, 2d ed., revised and unabridged (New York: Macmillan, 1959), 79.

MORE BOOKS BY
ERWIN W. LUTZER

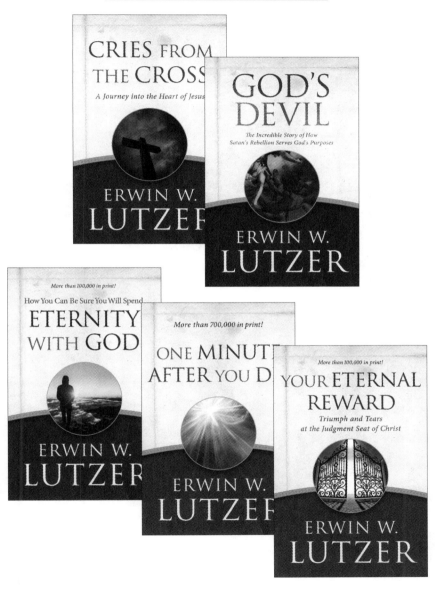

CRIES FROM THE CROSS
A Journey into the Heart of Jesus
ERWIN W. LUTZER

GOD'S DEVIL
The Incredible Story of How Satan's Rebellion Serves God's Purposes
ERWIN W. LUTZER

More than 100,000 in print!
How You Can Be Sure You Will Spend
ETERNITY WITH GOD
ERWIN W. LUTZER

More than 700,000 in print!
ONE MINUTE AFTER YOU DIE
ERWIN W. LUTZER

More than 100,000 in print!
YOUR ETERNAL REWARD
Triumph and Tears at the Judgment Seat of Christ
ERWIN W. LUTZER

MOODY Publishers™
From the Word to Life

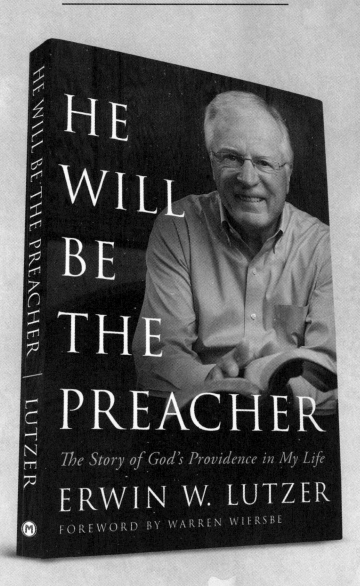

From the Word *to Life*

Moody Radio produces and delivers compelling programs filled with biblical insights and creative expressions of faith that help you take the next step in your relationship with Christ.

You can hear Moody Radio on 36 stations and more than 1,500 radio outlets across the U.S. and Canada. Or listen on your smartphone with the Moody Radio app!

www.moodyradio.org